I AM THAT I AM

A tribute to Sri Nisargadatta Maharaj who asks us to discard
all and stay in *I AM*–that contains the entire world,
the last progress being to transcend this very *I AMNESS* and
establish in the ultimate.

I AM THAT I AM

A Tribute to
Sri Nisargadatta Maharaj

S TEPHEN H. W OLINSKY

New Age Books

ISBN: 81-7822-262-0

First Indian Edition: Delhi, 2006
First Published 2000, USA

© 2000 by Stephen Wolinsky

Published by
NEW AGE BOOKS
A-44 Naraina Phase-I
New Delhi-110 028 (INDIA)
Email: nab@vsnl.in
Website: www.newagebooksindia.com

Printed in India
at Shri Jainendra Press
A-45 Naraina Phase-I, New Delhi-110 028

THE WORD THAT
IN THE STATEMENT REFERS TO EVERYTHING
THAT IS IN THE TOTALITY.

NISARGADATTA MAHARAJ

(Pg. 24, *The Nectar of the Lord's Feet,*)

DEDICATION

To Avadhut Nityananda
To the memory of Sri Nisargadatta Maharaj

Avadhut Nityananda appeared to "me" in the mid-1970s and initiated me. In 1996, Alexander Smit (a student of Nisargadatta Maharaj) said he had spoken to Maharaj about Nityananda:

Alexander Smit to
Nisargadatta Maharaj: "Did you ever meet Nityananda?"

Nisargadatta Maharaj: "Yes."

Alexander Smit: "What did you think of him?"

Nisargadatta Maharaj: "There is not a day which goes by that I don't think of him."

In this way, for "me" Nityananda brought me to Nisargadatta Maharaj, and it was through him that a place was provided for me to live for free in India with one of Nityananda's major disciples, Baba Muktananda, who lived just three hours away.

This tribute to Sri Nisargadatta Maharaj represents the fruit of that initiation.

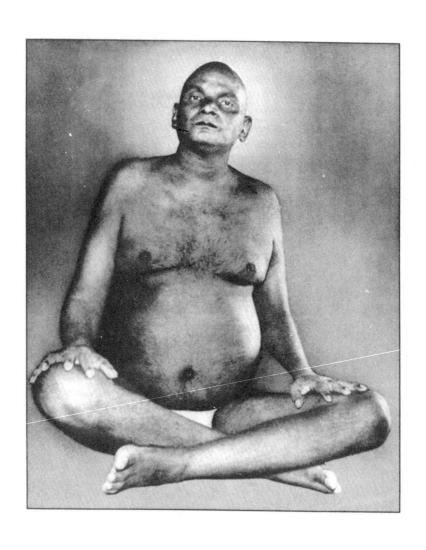

AVADHUT NITYANANDA

ACKNOWLEDGEMENTS

Carolina Carolanda, my divine Leni
Allen Horne, Editorial Assistance
Marylu Erlandson, Word processing

Robert Powell: For his time and energy in editing the *Ultimate Medicine*, *The Experience of Nothingness*, and *The Nectar of Immortality*.

Jean Dunn: For taping Nisargadatta Maharaj and editing *Seeds of Consciousness*, *Prior to Consciousness*, and *Consciousness and the Absolute*.

Ramesh Balsakar: A disciple of Nisargadatta Maharaj who continues to make himself available for questions, answers, and for *Pointers From Nisargadatta Maharaj*.

Alexander Smit: A Guru brother from Holland, who will be missed for his caring and direct teaching of Nisargadatta Maharaj.

Meinhard Van de Reep (Altamira Press, Holland) and Alexander Smit for providing me with many of the pictures contained within this book.

TABLE OF CONTENTS

THE SEARCH FOR REALITY IS THE MOST DANGEROUS OF ALL UNDERTAKINGS FOR IT DESTROYS THE WORLD IN WHICH YOU LIVE.

NISARGADATTA MAHARAJ

(PG. 495, I AM THAT)

The search for reality destroys more than that. For in its pursuit, it destroys the meaning and illusionary purpose that this world has come to mean to "you." Even more so, it destroys all images, lenses, and frames of reference. In a word, it destroys all you think or imagine yourself to be.

PROLOGUE

How does one even begin to write such a **tribute**? After having spent over six years in India and meeting some 50-60 teachers, gurus and meditation masters, "I" can unequivocally say that there were none who could compare to Sri Nisargadatta Maharaj. Why? Because there are those who have access to **THAT** or have "*Realized* themselves," and those who could teach. The combination of both the *realization* of **THAT** and the ability to teach is both rare and unique. This "I" saw only in Sri Nisargadatta Maharaj. I do not wish to diminish anyone else, but it must be understood that *realization does not mean teaching ability*. Nisargadatta Maharaj had both, and *without* compromise, *without* wanting anything from anyone, *without* attempting to create an organization, *without* creating the illusion of a mission, *without* desiring name or fame, *without* trying to win a popularity contest, *without* the desire to *be* anyone or anything, *without* wanting to teach or be a teacher, *without* the need to be the center of attention, and having been cured of the disease of the desire of wanting to be a Guru. He never *referred to himself* as a Mahatma, Bagawan, or a Paramahansa, and founded no school and no philosophy. He merely spoke about what "he" "himself" had "experienced", without falling for any of the spiritual trappings or games. Instead, he dared to tread on every concept we hold dear and sacred, in his attempt to push us through and beyond concepts.

MY WORDS, AS KNOWLEDGE, IF PLANTED IN YOU, WILL REMOVE ALL OTHER WORDS, ALL CONCEPTS.

NISARGADATTA MAHARAJ

(Pg. 9, The Ultimate Medicine)

"I" told a friend recently that when "I" look at the picture of Nisargadatta Maharaj in *I AM THAT* I feel humbled and over whelmed with awe, and gratitude, so much so that words themselves pale in significance and do not reach the depth of "my" feeling.

I first was introduced to *I AM THAT* upon my arrival in India in about January of 1977. Although "I" was deeply moved by the profound clarity of the books (then two volumes), "I" made only a very feeble and unsuccessful attempt to see him then.

Around January 31 (my birthday), 1979, however, I was able to see him and talk with him for the first time.

Much of those dialogues, interactions, and confrontations that occurred between us have been documented in earlier works. Nisargadatta Maharaj asked me to stay eight days and absorb the teachings. On the eighth day his words gave me all I might ever need to know. He began pacing back and forth, and then he turned to me and ferociously shouted:

"YOU'VE BEEN AROUND LONG ENOUGH, YOU SHOULD KNOW BY NOW, THERE IS NO BIRTH, THERE IS NOT DEATH, THERE IS NO PERSON. IT IS ALL A CONCEPT, IT'S ALL AN ILLUSION!

AND SO NOW YOU KNOW
THE NOTHING, AND SO
NOW YOU CAN LEAVE!"

Although it took twelve years to realize its truth, and although until his death I got to see him and interact with him only about twenty-five times or so, as Jean Dunn said, in *Prior to Consciousness* each sentence which Nisargadatta Maharaj uttered was an Upanishad.

Sometimes he let me stay, sometimes he told me to go.

Almost twenty years after his death, my gratitude and overwhelming humility toward him are always with me as "I" realized the truth of his words - **"IT'S CLOSER THAN YOUR NEXT BREATH."**

After the publication of the *Way of the Human* trilogy, "I" began very spontaneously to put together dialogues of questions and answers that were asked of him. Somehow what it turned into however, was a *Tribute to Sri Nisargadatta Maharaj.* As "I" reread *I AM THAT*, twelve or more times, "I" realized all that had come to pass, or that "I" had imagined had arisen within this "me" in the form of Quantum Psychology, as well as everything else for that matter, including **I AM** and **Beyond**, had come through Sri Nisargadatta Maharaj and the realization of his words.

WORDS OF A REALIZED MAN NEVER MISS THEIR PURPOSE. THEY WAIT FOR THE RIGHT CONDITIONS TO ARISE WHICH MAY TAKE SOME TIME, AND THIS IS NATURAL, FOR THERE IS A SEASON FOR SOWING AND A SEASON FOR HARVESTING. BUT THE WORD OF THE GURU IS A SEED THAT CANNOT PERISH.

NISARGADATTA MAHARAJ

(Pg. 421-422, I Am That)

To appreciate this, for years "I" thought, that I had something to do with the creation of Quantum Psychology. I discovered that "I" had nothing to do with it, nor did it belong to a "me"; rather it was, as he had said to me on two occasions: "**MY WORDS ARE TRUE, SO THEY MUST COME TRUE**," and, "**IT WILL BE REVEALED TO YOU**."

I grasped the significance of this when I realized that his words were like seeds which he had planted, and with proper watering and luck, they would bear fruit whose growth would be as unstoppable as the rising of the sun.

In September 1999, I saw an image arise out of the pure NOTHINGNESS; a scripted title, A TRIBUTE TO SRI NISARGADATTA MAHARAJ. Of course, he needs no tribute nor does an "I", so we could call it a tribute to **THAT**, or the inner SELF or GURU, knowing of course that a title is only a descriptive representation and certainly Sri Nisargadatta Maharaj was beyond description.

I AM NOT DESCRIBABLE
NOR DEFINABLE.

NISARGADATTA MAHARAJ
(Pg. 520 I Am That)

What was extraordinary about Maharaj was his constant instruction.

TO DISCOVER WHO YOU ARE,
YOU MUST FIRST DISCOVER WHO YOU ARE NOT.

NISARGADATTA MAHARAJ

What is even more shocking, looking back in hindsight, is that it was exactly like he had said: "**IT HAPPENS ON ITS OWN - THERE IS NO DOER OF IT**." Once this is completely imbibed, "you" realize not only who he was and is, (or wasn't and isn't); but, simultaneously, who you are (or aren't), which, as he said, is not "**PERCEIVABLE or CONCEIVABLE**."

To write such a piece can only be verbally described as profoundly moving. But even these words do not reach the core of what it was and is to "me".

In *Consciousness and the Absolute* by Jean Dunn, Nisargadatta Maharaj was asked, Do you think about your disciples? "He" replied, "More than you can ever know." In "my" experience, as strange as it may sound, "I" feel the non-verbal presence **I AM** and Nisargadatta Maharaj as pure **VOID THAT** is continually with "me." However, as not to omit or sugar-coat anything, many times the confrontation with Nisargadatta Maharaj was painful, for certainly he was not a passive sweet little **mahatma**. Still, his teaching style was relentless, non-compromising and "his" overwhelming presence has never left.

Nobody I had ever met could plant within "you" the seeds of *realization* - a seed, which as it grew, destroyed all other concepts. Nobody could so ably, without censoring or societal concerns, with total force and abandon, confront and *force* you to look at, question, and dismantle your concepts without having any mercy for your beliefs.

I WANT TO BLAST ALL CONCEPTS AND ESTABLISH YOU IN A NO-CONCEPT STATE.

NISARGADATTA MAHARAJ

I am reluctant to say much more other than that his words were so true, they destroyed and removed everything in their path - in other words, all of the "I"'s "I" thought "I" was. For although the direct confrontation *appeared* to come from outside, it actually came from "inside" for Nisargadatta Maharaj was the **INNER SELF** and **THAT**.

SADHANA (SPIRITUAL PRACTICE) IS THE WORK OF THE INNER SELF ON THE OUTER SELF.

NISARGADATTA MAHARAJ

So, "I" came to see that the creation, sustaining, and destruction of "me" and the illusion of Quantum Psychology existed for the dismantling of Stephen H. Wolinsky; and, if, by some chance it helped somebody else, that was fine. For Quantum Psychology was about confronting the "I" that imagines it is, so that its reality and falseness can arise "on-screen," and be seen for what it is, so that it can evaporate. Although painful, its results are inevitable;

ANYONE COMING HERE WILL BE LIQUIDATED.

NISARGADATTA MAHARAJ
(Pg. 30, The Ultimate Medicine)

What came to be realized was that the concept of an individual self, and what that self believes, are actually one and the same. In other words the "I" and the concept that you imagine you have, are one and the same. To illustrate, if there is a concept called "I am bad," the "I" appears to be separate from the concept, "I am bad" *BUT* actually the "I" which imagines it is separate from the concept is actually *in* the concept itself. In other words, "I am bad" appears as though there is a separate "I" which *has* the concept "I am bad." But in reality the "I" is in, and part of, the concept "I am bad." In this way, as a concept is destroyed through confrontation and enquiry so the "I" that one thinks one is, is also annihilated.

THIS IS A PLACE
WHERE THE INTELLECT GETS ANNIHILATED. . . .
THE EXPERIENCER TOO ALONG WITH THE
EXPERIENCE ARE BOTH
TO BE DISSOLVED.

NISARGADATTA MAHARAJ

A question is often asked, "why so much emphasis on confrontation?" The answer is, because it is only through **DIRECT CONFRONTATION** that the "I" concepts can be brought "on screen" or "on line," in other words, brought to the surface, questioned and gone beyond. If a "teacher," plays someone's game or lets someone get away with their unconscious self-deceptions because of the "teacher's" needs or desires, then the student unfortunately "gets no-where." Without direct intense confrontation, students can and will only continue to "act-out" their psychology. Why? Because that is all they can do.

So, Maharaj, the Inner Self, could hold a mirror up to your face, showing you *all* of what you did not want to look at;

IN ORDER TO LET GO OF SOMETHING YOU
MUST FIRST KNOW WHAT IT IS.

NISARGADATTA MAHARAJ

For this confrontation the word gratitude seems silly. For with the disappearance or evaporation of the observ*er* and know*er*, which arise and subside together **I AM THAT** is revealed, so with awe and humility. To **THAT** "I" pranam.

THE OBSERVER AND HIS OBSERVATION, AS WELL AS THE WORLD OBSERVED, APPEAR AND DISAPPEAR TOGETHER.

BEYOND IT ALL, THERE IS VOID. THIS VOID IS ONE FOR ALL.

(PG. 378, I AM THAT)

Nisargadatta Maharaj continually spoke of how rare it was for someone to understand his teachings. His words were so profound, that, to this day, "I" marvel at their **DIRECTNESS** and **POWER**. Nisargadatta Maharaj confronted "me" when he said that most people were more interested in community, finding friends, being a teacher, starting a spiritual business, or developing some kind of spiritual life style. He once said to me, with great disdain, *"I DON'T CARE IF YOU ARE SATISFIED OR PACIFIED WITH YOUR SPIRITUAL LIFE (WITH GREAT DISGUST), DO YOU KNOW YOURSELF?"* For Nisargadatta Maharaj, most people were truly not interested and certainly unwilling to *pay the price* of confronting everything without resolve and letting nothing stand in the way of finding out **WHO THEY ARE**; or, better said, finding out that **THEY ARE NOT**. For this reason, with reckless abandon, he did not play the societal game of nice, consciously censoring his words so the "other" could get it. He knew these behavior modifications were based upon the "teacher's" desire to be seen a certain way or liked, and hence it was motivated by the "teacher's need not the student's. Instead, spontaneously, he destroyed every concept in the way.

MY TALKS ARE NOT MEANT FOR NORMAL HUMAN BEINGS

(Pg. 42, Consciousness and the Absolute)

This book represents a **TRIBUTE TO SRI NISARGA-DATTA MAHARAJ**, what he meant to "me" and its *realization*. "I" did my best to leave "me" out of it, and hence "I" only discuss "myself" in order to clarify or deepen the understanding of the process. The book is divided into three main sections:1) his primary statements; 2) a short commentary; and (3) sometimes either a process or an edited question and answer session with "me," to elaborate upon or "experience" (*apperceive*) Nisargadatta Maharaj's words and their "meaning."

Apprehending or apperceiving can best be described as being aware of, or getting something without the use of, the perceptual apparatus.

APPERCEIVE OR APPREHENSION

Since we will be using Nisargadatta Maharaj's words of apperceive(ing) or apprehend(ing) throughout, "I" thought it important to include their Latin derivatives. The Latin root is *ad* plus *pericipere*, which occurs through a process of assimilation, being together with (one with), to seize, tackle, become aware of, to take possession of. (Please note these later edited dialogues from the United States and Europe arose for further discussion and/or had been omitted in early works.)

These words are difficult, if not impossible, when covering such topics - they are made available here for clarification so that as "I" renounce psychology and go beyond the concept of Quantum Psychology; or; better said, the "I" that was and is psychology and Quantum Psychology evaporates and disappears at least what had transpired can be made available. In hindsight, they can be used to view from a distance what appeared to occur. For even as Quantum Psychology and its "I" evaporates and disappears even the concept of **I AM, ENLIGHTENMENT, REALIZATION** and even the concept of a **BEYOND** too dissolves and evaporates, because all of these concepts requires a place, thing, location, or an event in space time, which is a **MIRAGE** and **IS NOT**.

Enjoy the ride with love

Your brother,
    Stephen
        September 1999

Introduction

NISARGADATTA MARARAJ— THE ROUGH GUIDE

· ·

When I was first introduced to **I AM THAT** and even with "personal" interactions with Nisargadatta Maharaj, the **I AM** seemed unclear and difficult to remain stabilized in. Unlike many "spiritual teachers," Nisargadatta Maharaj did not spoon feed you, allow you to be a baby, or baby you. He did not hold your hand and gently walk you through giving a specific Sadhana (spiritual practice) or deliver the information in a "nice" way. Rather, he threw you into the water, which you had been avoiding for so long, and you sank or swam on "your" own. For some, "I" imagine, this was pleasurable, for "me" it was both pleasurable and extremely painful and confrontive.

But like a moth flying into the flame, after "seeing" and going through the initial confrontation, I could not help continuing to fly into the flame of his confrontation. Like Icarus in the *myth of the minotaur,* who tried to escape the labyrinth (of the mind) on wings made of wax which melted when he flew to close to the sun so that he crashed down into the ocean (**THAT ONE SUBSTANCE**), "I", too, attempted to fly away on the false wax wings of my concepts. However, while flying to close to the light and sun of Nisargadatta Maharaj, the False Self melted and burned and "I" came crashing down into the ocean of **THAT ONE SUBSTANCE**. What is the message of Nisargadatta Maharaj? Continually over the years. I have been asked, "What was the practice, what was the sadhana?" I would say, "Stay in the **I AM** and discard all else. This **I AM** is the gateway or portal which draws one into **THAT**. This was the practice; however, what does this mean, and how does it take root?

NOW WHAT YOU HAVE LEARNED HERE BECOMES THE SEED.YOU MAY FORGET IT—APPARENTLY. BUT IT WILL AND IN DUE SEASON SPROUT, GROW, AND BEAR FLOWERS AND FRUIT. ALL WILL HAPPEN BY ITSELF.

NISARGADATTA MAHARAJ
(PG. 242, I AM THAT)

NISARGADATTA MAHARAJ AND ADVAITA-VEDANTA MADE SIMPLE

ADVAITA	*VEDANTA*
There is only **THAT ONE SUBSTANCE** not two or more substances	Neti-Neti
	(Sanskrit for Not This-Not this)

SUMMARY OF NISARGA (THE NATURAL) YOGA;

1) There is only **ONE SUBSTANCE**.
2) What you know about yourself came from outside of you, therefore discard it.
3) Question everything, do not believe anything.
4) In order to find out who you are, you must first find out who you are not.
5) In order to let go of something, you must first know what it is.
6) The experiencer is contained within the experience itself.
7) Anything you think you are—you are **NOT**.
8) Hold onto the **I AM**, let go of everything else.
9) Anything you know about you cannot be.

Once Nisargadatta Maharaj asked a student, "Who told you that you exist?" After some silence Maharaj said, "Consciousness tells you that you exist, and you believe it. If you understand just this—it is enough." If you understand this, you need not read any further. For as Maharaj said, "Understanding is all that can be given."

With Love Again
    Your brother,
        Stephen

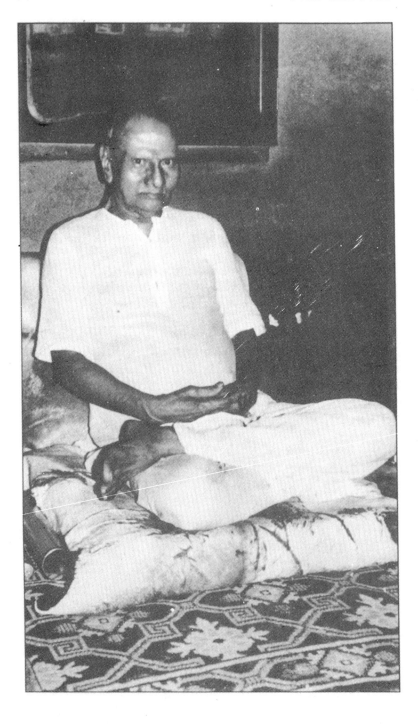

One

THE I AM

. . . .

THE IN-DWELLING PRINCIPLE
"YOU ARE" WITHOUT WORDS
THAT ITSELF YOU ARE.

NISARGADATTA MAHARAJ
(Pg. 138, the ultimate medicine)

THE I AM MADE EASY

ONE WHO IS COMPLETELY RID
OF ONE'S VERY OWN CONCEPT OF I AM
IS COMPLETELY LIBERATED.

(PG. 203, SEEDS OF CONSCIOUSNESS)

What is the **I AM**? To begin with, according to Nisargadatta · Maharaj, the **I AM** has two levels. The first is the *Verbal I AM*.

THE VERBAL I AM

According to Nisargadatta Maharaj, the *verbal I AM* is all you can say about yourself after you say, **I AM**. All else after this verbal **I AM** is to be discarded. If you witness "your" "internal" dialogue, notice that a verbal **I AM** must precede statements you make about yourself. All else, after this verbal **I AM,** cannot be true, and hence must be discarded. .

There are two reasons why anything that is thought or said about one's self after **I AM** or about another after **YOU ARE** is untrue? To illustrate, first there is the quantum level, unseen by the nervous system. So, too, the microscopic level is unseen by the nervous system. Sensation is recorded by the nervous system and the brain *prior* to the thought **I AM** *(fill in the blank)* , or **YOU ARE** *(fill in the blank)* . All you say about yourself or another arises in the cerebral cortex after the nervous system has already omitted billions of stimuli and has selected out only a fraction of these stimuli to deduce and conclude "after the fact," **I AM** this or that, or **YOU ARE** this or that. Those conclusions about one's self or another occur much later after the experience has already taken place and hence eliminates most of the information about *what is*.

Second, the **I AM** is a condensation, or a primal vibration, of **UNDIFFERENTIATED CONSCIOUSNESS**, and as such, although it remains **UNDIFFERENTIATED CONSCIOUS-NESS**, the **I AM** does not see its source as **UNDIFFERENTI-ATED CONSCIOUSNESS** also it cannot view the quantum level.

In this way, Nisargadatta Maharaj called the **I AM** and its reflected world a *pinprick*.

THE NON-VERBAL I AM

The Non-Verbal I AM: **The I AM is the glue of individuality, and the primal illusion which holds the *mirage* together.**

Stephen Wolilnsky

The non-verbal I AM has no thoughts, memory, emotions, associations, perceptions, attention or intentions and is the GATE-WAY and touchstone to the NOTHINGNESS. *The Non-Verbal I AM* is the *stateless state or No-State state*, that is prior to the verbal **I AM.** It is what is "when" you do not use your thoughts, memory, emotions, associations, perceptions, attention or intentions. That blank *stateless state* or *No-State state* is the non-verbal **I AM.** Nisargadatta Maharaj would say, "Hold onto the **I AM**, let go of everything else." This is because the non-verbal **I AM** is the first emanation of **CONSCIOUSNESS**, and when it is stayed with, it acts as a gateway or portal to the absolute **NOTHINGNESS** or **PURE UNDIFFERENTIATED CONSCIOUSNESS.**

The I AM is a portal or gateway that, when stayed with, dissolves or evaporates as the **BIG EMPTINESS** or **UNDIFFER-ENTIATED CONSCIOUSNESS** is revealed.

BE IN THAT BEINGNESS THEN IT WILL TELL YOU HOW BEINGNESS TURNS INTO NON-BEINGNESS

NISARGADATTA MAHARAJ
(Pg. 5, Nectar of the Lord's Feet)

By staying in the gateway, **I AM,** the **CONSCIOUSNESS**, which the **I AM** is made of, absorbs the **I AM** like a dry sponge absorbs water.

THE I AM'S REFLECTOR-REFLECTION— I-DENTIFICATION DEVICE

The Reflector-Reflection - I-dentification device is a way to describe the process of the **I AM**. **CONSCIOUSNESS** through the **I AM** (which is **COMPACTED CONSCIOUSNESS**) reflects out a thought, for example, and then **CONSCIOUSNESS** "moves forward," fusing, condensing, and identifying itself with this "I" thought, when in reality, the **I AM** and the thought, object, person, and world, are a reflection of and made of the same substance as the **CONSCIOUSNESS,** which uses the **I AM** as its lens.

THE I AM IS THE WORLD; IT CONTAINS THE ENTIRE WORLD.

NISARGADATTA MAHARAJ

(Pg. 191, The Ultimate Medicine)

THE I AM IS THE GURU

The I AM is the Guru, God, or deity of worship. The outer Guru or deity is the **I AM**. When **CONSCIOUSNESS** through the **I AM** projects out, a diety appears as an object of worship. Actually, **CONSCIOUSNESS** through the **I AM** reflects out a God, Guru, or deity, assumes it is separate from itself, and then gives its reflection power and worships it. How does this apply to Bhakti Yoga (the yoga of devotion)? What is the goal of Bhakti Yoga? It is when the lov*er* and the belov*ed* (object of worship) are one. In this way the goal of Bhakti Yoga is realized when you stay and **BE** the **I AM**, which is the lens of the deity of worship.

THE I AM IS MADE
OF CONSCIOUSNESS

The I AM is made of CONSCIOUSNESS, and so is everything else. By staying in the **I AM**, its fundamental nature as **CONSCIOUSNESS** is revealed.

The I AM is the first permutation and appearance *of* **UNDIFFERENTIATED CONSCIOUSNESS**. In this way the **I AM** is the glue which holds this *mirage* world together. Simply stated, no **I AM**, *no you, no you, no your world.*

THE I AM IN DEPTH

THE I AM AS THE
REFLECTOR-REFLECTION

The **I AM** as condensed **CONSCIOUSNESS** acts as a lens through which **CONSCIOUSNESS** reflects. The **I AM** is like a magnifying glass, and the sun or **CONSCIOUSNESS** through the magnifying glass of condensed **CONSCIOUSNESS** called **I AM** reflects out light. This reflected projection of **CONSCIOUSNESS** through the **I AM**, once identified with, forms the "I" and the world in which we live. The **I AM** and its reflected appearances give the illusion that there are two or more substances separate from the **I AM** and **CONSCIOUSNESS**. In this way **CONSCIOUSNESS** through the **I AM** reflects out thoughts, etc., and acts as the glue which holds the entire illusionary world together. The reflections of **CONSCIOUSNESS** through the **I AM,** when identified with, become the *major veil* that covers the pure (no subject-object) **I AM**, and the **CONSCIOUSNESS** of which the **I AM** is made of. When the **I AM** is stayed with, or turned upon itself, it evaporates and is no longer. Then there is only pure **CONSCIOUSNESS** and the **ABSOLUTE**.

The question often arises, why is the **I AM** so difficult, or why is it so difficult to just stay in the **I AM** or just be **WHO YOU ARE**?

This can best be described as follows: The **CONSCIOUSNESS** through the **I AM**, with its Reflector-Reflection identification device makes it appear as though *"you"* have a thought called "I hate myself" or "I love myself." It makes it appear as though the thought arose, and is separate from the **I AM** and **CONSCIOUSNESS**.

In reality, **CONSCIOUSNESS** through the **I AM** reflected out the thought called "I hate myself" and then **CONSCIOUSNESS** identifies itself as that thought, thus losing the awareness of (itself) the **I AM** and **CONSCIOUSNESS**. This process acts like a film projector which projects a movie out on a screen, which if you identify with the reflection on the screen as "you" and "your life," you "lose" the **I AM**, and the light or **CONSCIOUSNESS** which the film is made of.

It is this pivotal understanding that **CONSCIOUSNESS** with the **I AM** as a vehicle and its automatic projection →reflection→identification makes it difficult to just stay with the **I AM**, rather than I-dentify oneself as being a reflection of **CONSCIOUSNESS** or **I AM**.

THIS MANIFEST WORLD IS CREATED BY THAT "I AMNESS" THE LAST PROGRESS WILL BE FOR YOU TO TRANSCEND THIS "I AMNESS" AND GET STABILIZED IN THE ULTIMATE

NISARGADATTA MAHARAJ
(Pg. 55, Seeds Of CONSCIOUSNESS)

What keeps this *mirage* alive? The **I AM**'s Reflector-Reflection identification process, which, if operative, the reflection (person) imagines it is separate from the **I AM** and **CONSCIOUSNESS**. As long as the **I AM**, with its Reflector-Reflection identification, is identified with as "I" the *mirage* remains solid.

THE I AM DECEPTION

CONSCIOUSNESS through the **I AM,** acts like a movie projector reflecting out a movie reflection world with characters, exerting an enormous power of deception in that it immediately makes you believe that **I AM** separate and **AM,** and **YOU ARE** separate and **ARE,** when *you are not.*

It can best be illustrated as follows: **CONSCIOUSNESS** through the **I AM** (compacted consciousness) movie projector projects a thought, which contains within it an "I" which identifies itself as real and *not* just a projected reflection. It would be like the reflection in a mirror believing it is separate, alive, and exists independently of you. In the same way, the reflection, thoughts, beliefs, images, etc., believe they are real and separate from the **I AM,** not realizing that the **I AM** and **CONSCIOUSNESS** is the source of them, and without the **I AM** they would vanish

This **CONSCIOUSNESS→I AM** projector reflector→reflection→identification is almost instantaneous.

When you stay in **I AM,** its reflections and concepts are seen for what they are and they are absorbed into its source, the **I AM** and **CONSCIOUSNESS.**

To illustrate imagine you are looking in a mirror and suddenly you think you are the reflection in the mirror. "You" (as subject **I AM** looking in the mirror) are no more, rather there is an identification with the reflection in the mirror, which is now called "I", and which you now call yourself. When this occurs, the awareness of the **I AM** (your inner self) disappears.

To review even deeper; there is no separate thinker, feeler or sensor. The thinker, feeler, and sensor, are contained within the thought, feeling, or sensation itself, and are reflections of **CONSCIOUSNESS** through the vehicle of the **I AM** (which is also made of **CONSCIOUSNESS).**

THE I AM: REFLECTOR-REFLECTION PROCESS AND TIME

The concept of the past is an illusion. Each moment, thoughts, images, and memories which are made of **CONSCIOUSNESS** appear as reflections through the **I AM.** Contained within each *projected reflection* is a memory or idea of a self, an "I" and

"me" with a past, a present and a future. Thi creates the illusion of
a *me* in present time. Also contained within this thought/memory
projected reflection is its emotional component. Even more strik-
ing is the fact that contained within each thought-memory-emo-
tion is the projected-reflection's illusion that there is a cause and
an effect, or reason, for why they are here. This contains the implicit concept called "**I am here**." When this is coupled with the
concept of a past, present, and future glued together by the **I AM,**
it creates an enormously powerful "I" reflection. It makes this illu-
sory "I" believe *it is*, and that it is separate and independent. In
other words, the reflection of "I" now believes that something happened in a past time, which thus justifies this "present time" experience, when in reality, there is no past time or even present. Both
are contained within the *mirage's* illusion of time. Time only exists
within the thought-memory-emotion-me-past as a projected reflection of **CONSCIOUSNESS** through the **I AM,** it does not exist
"outside" of this.

It is like an image which arises and subsides in **NOTH-
INGNESS** and within it contains the **I AM** illusion, which
Nisargadatta Maharaj said, acts as a "**SEED FOR CONSCIOUS-
NESS.**" The alleged *now* does not reside in some present moment
– but rather within the concept of the reflection or reflected "I"
itself.

CONSCIOUSNESS through the **I AM** acts as a projector-reflector. You are beyond both and not it, nor even the observer
or witness of it. Because the concept of experiencing, and even
observing *are* also contained within the thought-memory-emotion-
body-self of the **I AM's** projector-reflector process, that makes the
movie and its characters seem real. This **I AM,** of no thoughts,
memory, emotions, associations, perceptions, attention, or intentions, is made of **CONSCIOUSNESS.** This "now" is there, but it
contains the illusion of the past.

QUESTION: I REMEMBER HAVING IT YESTERDAY TOO!

MARARAJ: THE MEMORY OF YES-TERDAY IS *NOW* ONLY.

QUESTION: BUT SURELY I EXIST IN
            TIME. I HAVE A PAST AND
            A FUTURE.

MAHARAJ: THAT IS *NOW* YOU IMAG-
            INE *NOW*.

QUESTION: THERE MUST HAVE BEEN
            A BEGINNING?

MAHARAJ: *NOW*

(PG. 134, I AM THAT)

DISMANTLING THE I AM REFLECTOR-REFLECTION IDENTIFICATION PROCESS

ENQUIRY

Below are contained an enquiry whose aim is to confront the very root of the projected-reflection of the *mirage* **I AM**. Becoming introverted, the **I AM** turns upon the **I AM** itself and into itself so that ultimately it too dissolves or evaporates.

ENQUIRY OVERVIEW
PART I
1) Where in or around the body is the **I AM**'s Reflector-Reflection identification device
2) If what is seen "inside" (i.e., thoughts or images, etc.) or "outside" (people, subjects, etc.) is a reflection of **CONSCIOUSNESS** through the **I AM**

- and made of the same **CONSCIOUSNESS** as **I AM** - what is the *apperceived*?

PART II

1) Notice that there is an appearance that the **I AM** is separate from the **I AM's** reflection.
2) If the **I AM** is separate from its reflection notice the experience.
3) What concept might have gotten the **I AM** to believe it was separate from its reflection?
4) If this were just a concept of **CONSCIOUSNESS** through the **I AM** and had nothing to do with anything_____?
5) What seductive pretense could the "I" reflect*ion*, which is identified with, use to get the **I AM** to believe it?
6) If the **I AM** and its reflect*ion* was not you _____?
7) If the **I AM** was a prism that reflected a solid form of the "light" or **CONSCIOUSNESS,** and you are not the prism or its reflected form, what is *apperceived*?

ENQUIRY

Demonstration:

Below is a edited *enquiry*. The Enquiry is placed here to enhance the capacity, give insight, and demonstrate an *enquiry* into the nature of **I AM**.

Wolinsky: Where in or around the body is the **I AM**?

Student: The space in front of this body.

Wolinsky: Notice that there is an appearance that the **CONSCIOUSNESS I AM** is separate from its reflection.

Student: Yes.

Note:

Here we first recognize the reflector tendency of
CONSCIOUSNESS through the **I AM** to make
the reflection appear separate from itself. Next we
get that they are the same substance.

Wolinsky: If **CONSCIOUSNESS** through the **I AM** is sepa-
             rate from its reflection notice the experience.

Student: I feel separate, like I am in a separate location.

Wolinsky: What concept might have gotten **CONSCIOUS-
             NESS** through the **I AM** to believe it was separate
             from its reflection?

Student: The **I AM** believed that it was not its reflection.

Wolinsky: If this were just a concept of the **I AM**, and had noth-
             ing to do with anything, what is the *apperception*?

Student: _____ Blank.

Note:

Often-times students go blank, as their concepts
disappear. Secondly, the **I AM,** along with its Reflection, which it I-dentifies with, is sometimes
attached to a physical inevitability like a heart beat,
eye blink, or breathing.

Wolinsky: Where on the body is the **I AM** and its reflector-
             reflection identification process attached?

Student: It is somehow attached to the eyes.

Wolinsky: What seductive pretense could the Reflector-Reflec-
             tion identification process use to get the **I AM** to
             believe it?

Student: It just does.

Wolinsky: If there is a separation between the **I AM** and its
                reflection device and the eyes what occurs?

Student: I feel blank, really gone - like I just want to fall into
                the **NOTHINGNESS**.

Wolinsky: If the **I AM** and its reflection is separate, what is the
                "experience" like?

Student: I feel separate and I feel located.

Note:
Here we are pointing to what occurs when the **I
AM** is separate from its reflection.

Wolinsky: If the **I AM** and its reflection are made of the same
                substance as **CONSCIOUSNESS** what occurs?

Student: I just am.

Wolinsky: If the **I AM** is separate from its reflection what does
                not occur?

Student: Merging, oneness.

Wolinsky: If the **I AM** and its reflection are the same substance,
                what does not occur?

Student: Location and separation.

Wolinsky: If the **I AM** and its refflection are the same substance
                or **CONSCIOUSNESS** what, if anything gets re-
                sisted?

Student: Nothing.

Wolinsky: If the **I AM** and its Reflector-Reflection identifica-
             tion process had nothing to do with anything, then
             _____?

Student: It is not me - I am not.

Wolinsky: If the **I AM** was like a prism that reflected a solid
             form of the "light" or **CONSCIOUSNESS**, and you
             are not the prism or the form, what is the *apprecep-
             tion*_____?

Student: _____Long silence.

Wolinsky: If what you see "inside" or "outside" is a reflection
             of **I AM** and made of the same **CONSCIOUSNESS**
             as **I AM**, then _____?

Student: _____Long silence.

ENQUIRY: THE I AM
AS CONSCIOUSNESS

OVERALL PROCESS

Closed Eyed I
1.   Notice a thought.
2.   Notice what occurs if the **I AM** and the thought
     are made of the same **CONSCIOUSNESS**.

Closed Eyed II
1.   Notice an emotion.
2.   Notice what occurs if the **I AM** and the emotion
     are made of the same **CONSCIOUSNESS.**

Open Eyed I
1.   Notice an object.
2.   Notice what occurs if the **I AM** and the object are
     made of the same **CONSCIOUSNESS.**

Open Eyed II
1. Notice a person.
2. Notice what occurs if the **I AM** and the object are
    made of the same **CONSCIOUSNESS.**

Don't be deceived by the **I AMNESS**, and its reflector-reflection – identification process which creates the illusion of this world, with its superficiality. Identification with the **I AM's** reflection creates, and is the veil which hides the **I AM** and the **CONSCIOUSNESS** of which the **I AM** is made.

The illusion of, or veil of separation between, **I AM** and its reflection must be pierced so that - **CONSCIOUSNESS,** or the substance of which the **I AM** and its reflection and all is made, can be revealed.

YOU MUST BECOME CONCEPT FREE. PUT THE AX TO THE CONCEPTS, INCLUDING THE CONCEPT "I AM"

NISARGADATTA MAHARAJ

The concept **I AM** serves as a gateway or portal to **THAT NOTHINGNESS, CONSCIOUSNESS.** However, as long as the **I AM** is present, the illusion that **CONSCIOUSNESS** is made of two or more substances persists. Once the **I AM** dissolves or evaporates only **THAT** remains.

THE BEINGNESS I AM IS A CLOAK OF ILLUSION OVER THE ABSOLUTE. IN OTHER WORDS, THE BEINGNESS, WHICH AS THE VERY FIRST AND PRIMARY CONCEPT I AM IS HALF THE CONCEPTUAL ILLUSION

NISARGADATTA MAHARAJ

(Pg. 40, Nectar of Immortality)

Although for many it might seem redundant, the **I AM** is the pivotal departure point in understanding Nisargadatta Maharaj.

"APPERCEIVING" THE I AM

How can one directly "experience" **I AM**. Use this brief process and allow someone to walk you through and notice what occurs.

Let your eyes close and notice what occurs when "**I**" (your partner) says:

Step I   Without using your thoughts, memory, emotions, associations, perceptions, attention or intentions, are you a man, woman or neither?

Step II   Without using your thoughts, memory, emotions, associations, perceptions, attention or intentions, do you exist, not exist or neither?

Step III   Without using your thoughts, memory, emotions, associations, perceptions, attention or intentions, are you perfect, imperfect or neither?

Step IV   Without using your thoughts, memory, emotions, associations, perceptions, attention or intentions, are you defined, undefined or neither?

Step V   Without using your thoughts, memory, emotions, associations, perceptions, attention or intentions, are you alone, connected or neither?

Step VI   Without using your thoughts, memory, emotions, associations, perceptions, attention or intentions, are you loving, unlovable or neither?

Step VII   Without using your thoughts, memory, emotions, associations, perceptions, attention or intentions, are you worthless, valuable or neither?

Step VIII   Without using your thoughts, memory, emo-
             tions, associations, perceptions, attention or in-
             tentions, are you perfect, imperfect or neither?

Step IX   Notice the stateless state of no thoughts,
             memory, emotions, associations, perceptions,
             attention or intentions.

**Notice the stateless state, the blank No-State state of
the Non-verbal I AM.**

Nisargadatta said, "All I can say is **I AM**." This is the verbal **I AM**. The Non-Verbal **I AM** is "prior" to this.

SADHANA (SPIRITUAL PRACTICE) IS A CONSISTENT ATTEMPT TO CROSS OVER FROM THE VERBAL TO THE NON-VERBAL.

NISARGADATTA MAHARAJ
(Pg., 435 I Am That)

Moving from the verbal **I AM** *(Fill in the blank)* to the
non-verbal **I AM** of no thoughts, memory, emotion, associations,
perceptions, attention, or intentions, is the introverted re-tracing
process which is sadhana (Spiritual practice).

"STAY IN THE I AM, LET GO OF EVERYTHING ELSE."

NISARGADATTA MAHARAJ

THE I AM AS GURU OR DEITY

SO LONG AS THE CONSCIOUSNESS IS THERE THE HUMMING GOES ON, AND WHO DOES THE HUMMING? THE PRINCIPLE WHICH IS HUMMING AND SAYING "I AM," "I AM" IS ITSELF YOUR GURU.

NISARGADATTA MAHARAJ
(Pg. 95, The Nectar of Immortality)

The **I AM** is the guru or the inner Self. In this way one can easily appreciate that the **I AM** is the guru and is you, and is always with you, (abide) in your own self the (**I AM**)

GURU – GURU – GURU THAT IS I AMNESS

NISARGADATTA MAHARAJ

The **I AMNESS**, without thoughts, memory, emotions, associations, perceptions, attention or intentions, is the **GURU**, **GOD** and the **INNER SELF**.

THE KNOWLEDGE OF I AM MEANS CONSCIOUSNESS, GOD, ISWARA, YOUR GURU, ETC. BUT YOU, THE ABSOLUTE, ARE NOT THAT.

NISARGADATTA MAHARAJ
(Pg. 128, The Nectar Of Immortality)

The **I AM** is **CONSCIOUSNESS, GOD, ISWARA, GURU,** etc. Once there is no longer an **I AM** (*Fill in the blank*) or even the non-verbal **I AM**; there is only the **ABSOLUTE**, and hence no **GOD** or **GURU**. In this way the **I AM** is the inner self or Guru. And it is **CONSCIOUSNESS** through the **I AM (which is condensed consciousness)**, which appears as an "outer" reflection—the "outer" deity or "outer" guru - which devotees and bhaktas' worship. To mediate on one's self is to be the **I AM** without using your thoughts memory, emotions, associations, perceptions, attention or intentions, and it is the goal of Bhakti yoga; i.e., when the beloved one (guru or deity) and you, the lover (the **I AM**), realize that they are **ONE**.

I AM: THE PRIMAL CONCEPT

THIS PRIMARY CONCEPT IS THE KNOWLEDGE OF "I AM." IT IS THE MOTHER OF ALL OTHER CONCEPTS. WHEN THIS CONCEPT IS THERE, THEN SO MANY OTHER CONCEPTS ALSO AP-PEAR. NOW, WHATEVER RELIGIONS THERE ARE, THEY ARE ONLY FULL OF CONCEPTS. SOMEBODY LIKES A PAR-TICULAR CONCEPT AND PASSES IT ON TO HIS DISCIPLES, AND HE GETS A FOLLOWING. BUT WITH THAT, THEY CANNOT GET ETERNAL PEACE OR SATISFACTION. IN ORDER TO GET THAT SATISFACTION, YOU MUST FIND THE SOURCE OF THIS PRIMARY CON-CEPT "I AM." AND ONCE YOU KNOW THAT, YOU CAN TRANSCEND IT. THEN YOU DO NOT HAVE ANYTHING TO

TELL THE WORLD, BECAUSE THE
WORLD WANTS ONLY FRAGMENTARY
MODIFICATIONS. THEY WANT ACTIVI-
TIES. SO THIS KNOWLEDGE WILL RE-
MAIN ONLY WITH YOU, AND THERE
WILL NOT BE MANY CUSTOMERS FOR
IT.

NISARGADATTA MAHARAJ
(Pg. 188, The Ultimate Medicine)

The **I AM** is the primal reference point from which experiences arise. No **I AM** - no experience.

The Non Verbal **I AM**, with no thoughts, memory, emotions associations, perceptions, attention, or intentions, is pure
beingness, *"prior"* to its reflection. The **I AM** is a by product of
UNDIFFERENTIATED CONSCIOUSNESS, or is made of **UN-
DIFFERENTIATED CONSCIOUSNESS** which appears as *differentiated* **CONSCIOUSNESS**. The **I AM** is the first movement
of **UNDIFFERENTIATED CONSCIOUSNESS.** It is therefore
the *Seed of CONSCIOUSNESS.* **CONSCIOUSNESS** through the
I AM projects out a reflection which appears "as if" it is separate
from **CONSCIOUSNESS** through the **I AM**; hence, the world and
"your" thoughts, psychology, knowing, etc., give the illusion of
being separate from the **I AM** when they are not.

"One" must begin to realize or *apperceive*, through confrontation, enquiry and investigation, that the **I AM,** which is a by-
product of **UNDIFFERENTIATED CONSCIOUSNESS** and its
projected reflection, is really only **THAT ONE SUBSTANCE** or
CONSCIOUSNESS. It is through direct investigation that not only
the object being investigated disappears—but also so does the in-
vestigator.

To go beyond the projected reflection of the **I AM** and its
projected reflection, i.e., the "I", the world, etc., must be *apperceived* as either *one* with the **I AM**, or the **I AM** itself must be held
onto, discarding all else. By staying with **I AM**, the reflection even-

tually evaporates. The former has been described to me by both Nisargadatta Maharaj and Baba Prakashananda as, "I have eaten the world, it is now inside of me." We could say they have re-absorbed the **I AM's** projected reflection by realizing they are made of the same **CONSCIOUSNESS**, so that the **I AM** is inside and with itself as **CONSCIOUSNESS**.

In the latter example you can hold onto the **CONSCIOUS-NESS** of **I AM,** or the **I AM** is "in" itself, and let go of its projected reflection, and just **BE I AM**. Ultimately, however, the **I AM** itself evaporates.

What does this mean? Within each experience is the non-verbal **I AM**. In other words, on the subtlest of subtle levels, the **I AM** is the seed and lens through which **CONSCIOUSNESS** projects out an image or reflection of what is seen, i.e., the "I" and all you identify with, is the reflection of **I AM**. However, the **I AM,** when stayed with, evaporates and leads to pure **BEINGNESS** - or beyond the **I AM** itself. How does this occur? When the **I AM** is gone beyond or begins to evaporate, awareness of the **BIG EMP-TINESS** is realized. To *apperceive* this, explore the **ENQUIRY** below:

BEYOND THE I AM

ENQUIRY

Enquiry Step I   Notice a thought.

Enquiry Step II   Be the **I AM** prior to the thought.

Enquiry Step III   Notice what occurs when "I" say what **I AM** is **I AMING** that (or what **I AM** is reflecting that). Notice the **CONSCIOUSNESS** beyond **I AMNESS** or the pure beingness or **CONSCIOUS-NESS I AM** is made of.

Enquiry Step IV   Allow your awareness to move,
                       fall or expand outward or back-
                       ward, becoming aware of the **BIG
                       EMPTINESS**. Notice how the
                       EMPTINESS *appears* to go on
                       forever.

Enquiry Step V   Allow the awar*er* of the **EMPTI-
                       NESS** to be the same substance
                       as the **BIG EMPTINESS**.

or variation

Enquiry Step V   *Variation*: Notice what occurs
                       when "I" say, "What awar*er* is
                       awaring that?"

MUKTANANDA AND NISARGADATTA MAHARAJ

Question: You spent a lot of time with Muktananda, yet he
                never spoke of this.

Stephen: He did, but in a more obscure way. His most impor-
                tant teaching might look like this:

                Meditate on yourself,
                Worship yourself,
                Kneel to yourself,
                Honor and worship your own being,
                God dwells within you as you.

Nisargadatta said the **I AM** is a by-product, a touchstone
between **THAT** unmanifest **CONSCIOUSNESS** and this manifest. The **I AM** is the self and is God. In this way, we can look at
Muktananda's teaching in the light of Nisargadatta Maharaj as follows:

Meditate on your self (**I AM**) = **BE** the **I AM**.
Worship your self (**I AM**) = **BE** the **I AM**.
Kneel to your self (**I AM**) = **BE** the **I AM**.
God (**I AM**) dwells within you (**I AM**) as you (**I AM**).

This hopefully helps to link the two.

THE I AM AND MEDITATION (DHYANA)

DHYANA IS WHEN THIS KNOWLEDGE, THIS CONSCIOUSNESS OF I AM MEDITATES ON ITSELF AND NOT ON SOMETHING OTHER THAN ITSELF.

NISARGADATTA MAHARAJ
(Pg. 86, The Ultimate Medicine)

When the **I AM** turns in on itself, there is pure (no subject-object) meditation. *Nisarga Yoga*, or the Natural Yoga, is pure Bhakti-Jnana-Dhyana yoga. When **I AM** is totally identified with, the fruit of **BHAKTI** (devotion) is realized. When all else is discarded, it is **JNANA** (no-dual knowledge), and when the subject of **I AM** becomes itself, there is **DHYANA** (meditation).

Words make it difficult to "get" or *apperceive* the **I AM** of no thoughts, memories, emotions, association, perceptions, attention or intentions. Once revealed, **I AM** is **I AM** only, and **I AM** no longer focuses on, identifies with, or believes in the reflections of **CONSCIOUSNESS**. Then the **I AM** evaporates like water in the air of **CONSCIOUSNESS**.

THIS KNOWLEDGE I AM SITS IN MEDITATION, BUT THIS KNOWLEDGE I AM, THIS CONSCIOUSNESS WHICH IS SITTING IN MEDITATION IS MEDITATING ON ITSELF. WHEN THIS CONSCIOUS-

NESS MERGES IN ITSELF THE STATE OF SAMADHI ENSUES. THEN, EVEN THE KNOWLEDGE I AM MEDITATING GETS LOST. SO THIS CONSCIOUS PRESENCE ALSO GETS MERGED INTO THE KNOWLEDGE OF THAT BEINGNESS –THIS IS SAMADHI

NISARGADATTA MAHARAJ

(Pg. 87, The Ultimate Medicine)

Who is meditating is always the question. *Is it an "I" trying to get something?* This is the true meaning of going within. It is being **I AM** and discarding all else, until the **I AM** turns on itself.

This **I AMNESS**, until it is investigated, automatically meditates or focuses on, and either becomes some projected reflection or *tries* to become some projected-reflection through a mantra, yantra, or tantra calling it spiritual. Although this does help to learn to focus the mind, the question always is, "Who is focusing on who or what?" Is the **I AM** focusing on its reflection? However, the **I AM**, by turning its attention around on the focus*er*, is realized. Is the **I AM** giving its power to its reflection "as if" the reflection were the source? This would be like a person who makes a statue of God and worships the statue, forgetting who made the statue. When the externally projected reflection drops away, only the **I AM** is. Soon, one realizes that the **I AM** is made solely of **CONSCIOUSNESS**. When the **CONSCIOUSNESS** "realizes" and stays in itself, there is *no-me or samadhi*. With no **I AM**, "me," or "I", only **CONSCIOUSNESS**, then the mediator-meditation is no longer. This is *no-me samadhi*.

BE IN THAT BEINGNESS, THEN IT
WILL TELL YOU HOW BEINGNESS TURNS
INTO NON-BEINGNESS

NISARGADATTA MAHARAJ
(Pg. 5, The Nectar Of Immortality)

By staying in the gateway **I AM,** then **CONSCIOUSNESS**
absorbs it like a dry sponge absorbs water.

THE KNOWER COMES AND GOES WITH THE
KNOWN, AND IS TRANSIENT, BUT THAT WHICH
KNOWS THAT IT DOES NOT KNOW, WHICH IS FREE
OF MEMORY AND ANTICIPATION, IS TIMELESS.

NISARGADATTA MAHARAJ
(Pg. 398, I Am That)

Question: Did Muktananda and Nisargadatta Maharaj meet?

Stephen: To my knowledge, no. However, a disciple of
               Nisargadatta Maharaj, Alexander Smit told me that
               he asked Nisargadatta Maharaj if he had ever met
               Bagawan Nityananda (Muktananda's guru). The con-
               versation went like this:

**Alexander Smit to Nisargadatta Maharaj: Did you ever meet
Nityananda (Muktananda's guru)?**

Nisargadatta Maharaj: Yes

Alexander Smit: What did you think?

Nisargadatta Maharaj: There is not a day which goes that I do not think of him (Nityananda).

THE LEVELS OF I AM ARE A MIRAGE

Question: You have talked about different levels of the **I AM**. How does it relate to ego?

Stephen: The Verbal **I AM**, and the Non Verbal **I AM** of no thoughts, memory, emotions, associations, perceptions, attention, or intentions, occurs from the body. This body "sense" **I AM** is a product of the nervous system and is chemical (see Chapter 3 The Body). The **I AM** is the gateway between the unmanifest and the manifest, it is the **INNER SELF**. And yet, it too is the seed a reflection of **CONSCIOUSNESS** as is the world and the "I." I don't mean this as negative. The **I AM** needs to be honored and worshipped - but if there is no body, then the chemicals could not come together to form **I AM** then there would be no **I AM**, and if there is no **I AM**, there is no vehicle for **CONSCIOUSNESS** to project through, and if there is no vehicle for **CONSCIOUSNESS** to project through, there is no ego.

When the **I AM** dissolves, the unmanifest and **WHO YOU ARE** are clearly there.

> *Do not fall into the trap that you are something or yes, "I" will discover* **WHO I AM**. *This will never occur because there is No-I, there is no "I" that you are.*
>   Stephen Wolinsky

The body and **I AM** are lenses. This lens views itself and makes the world appear as an "outer" world separate from itself. The "I" *which perceives the world is part of and is that lens or frame. You are not a lens or frame.*

Question: Where does the **I AM**-Body lens come from?

Stephen: The sense **I AM** at one level is a bio-chemical reaction so you cannot be a person. Chemicals come together and produce **I AM**. Ultimately, it does not arise from anywhere.

Question: But where does it come from then? Is it condensed **NOTHING**?

Stephen: This will shock you. The *I AM-Body is a mirage, a total illusion.* Everything discussed is a description.

Question: This does shock me. You mean I am an illusion, a *mirage*?

Stephen: Yes, like a projected image coming from a movie projector, made of shades of light, which you could call **CONSCIOUSNESS**. Like a character on a movie screen imagining it is real, has volition, preferences, and choices, not realizing it is all already in the script. The projected image might believe it can change its script or future outcome. But this too is in the movie. It would be like a character in a movie that dies at the end of two hours imagining during the movie that he can change that inevitable outcome. So too the character in the film believes **I AM** and **IT IS**. Through confrontation, enquiry and investigation, this too is seen as false. When Nisargadatta confronted "me", it brought up material so that "I" could enquire into it and investigate it, so that it would evaporate. *Once anything is investigated or enquired into, it disappears and evaporates.* The **I AM** and "you" neither arose nor subsided; it is a *mirage. You are a mirage which does not know it is a mirage.*

THIS I AMNESS IS THE
POWER OF MAYA

(Pg. 43, CONSCIOUSNESS and the Absolute)

The **I AMNESS** is the glue or first illusion of the projected image. It holds the character you imagine yourself to be on
the screen solid and together. Like a character on a screen made of
light, the character is made of **CONSCIOUSNESS**, and the "solidified" **CONSCIOUSNESS I AM** holds the *mirage* character
together. The **I AMNESS** is the first by-product of this illusion,
and, it is from this primal illusion (which Nisargadatta Maharaj
suggested is a gateway), from this **NOTHINGNESS** that the **I AM**
and the I-thou-other illusions arise.

THE I AM IS NOTHINGNESS
FROM NOTHINGNESS THIS
"I-AM-NESS" HAS APPEARED

NISARGADATTA MAHARAJ
(Pg. 147, the Nectar of Immortality)

The question is, "From where has the **I AMNESS** appeared?"

This can be answered as, the **I AMNESS** is condensed
EMPTINESS or **NOTHINGNESS**. The **NOTHINGNESS** is a
still spot within **UNDIFFERENTIATED CONSCIOUSNESS**,
like the eye of a hurricane.

The **I AM** is the gateway to **THAT**, and, by just staying
with the **I AM**, it evaporates and the **NOTHINGNESS** is revealed.

In order to *apperceive* this, allow someone to guide "you"
through this *ENQUIRY*.

Right now, let your eyes close, and notice what is apperceived;

Enquiry Step I   Without using your thoughts,
                                   memory, emotions, associations,
                                   perceptions, attention or intentions,
                                   are you a doer, a not doer, or nei-
                                   ther?

Enquiry Step II   Without using your thoughts,
                                   memory, emotions, associations,
                                   perceptions, attention or intentions,
                                   do you exist, not exist or neither?

Enquiry Step III   Without using your thoughts,
                                   memory, emotions, associations,
                                   perceptions, attention or intentions,
                                   what does existence or non-exist-
                                   ence even mean?

Enquiry Step IV   Without using your thoughts,
                                   memory, emotions, associations,
                                   perceptions, attention or intentions,
                                   are you in control, out of control,
                                   or neither?

Enquiry Step V   Without using your thoughts,
                                   memory, emotions, associations,
                                   perceptions, attention or intentions,
                                   are you complete, incomplete, or
                                   neither?

Enquiry Step VI   Without using your thoughts,
                                   memory, emotions, associations,
                                   perceptions, attention or intentions,
                                   what does complete or incomplete
                                   even mean?

Enquiry Step VII   Without using your thoughts,
                                   memory, emotions, associations,
                                   perceptions, attention or intentions,
                                   powerful, powerless or neither?

Enquiry Step VIII   Without using your thoughts,
                           memory, emotions, associations,
                           perceptions, attention or intentions,
                           what does powerful, or powerless
                           even mean?

Enquiry Step IX   Notice the stateless state "when"
                           "you" do not use "your" thoughts,
                           memory, emotions, associations,
                           perceptions, attention or intentions.

Enquiry Step X   Allow "your" awareness to move
                           expand or to fall backward notic-
                           ing the **BIG EMPTINESS**, now al-
                           low the awar*er* to be the same sub-
                           stance as the **BIG EMPTINESS**.

or

Enquiry Step X   *Variation*: Notice what occurs when
                           "I" say, what awar*er* is awaring that.

THE KNOWLEDGE I AM
IS NOTHING

NISARGADATTA MAHARAJ
(PG. 36, THE NECTAR OF IMMORTALITY)

The **I AM** is made of **NOTHINGNESS**, pure **CON-
SCIOUSNESS** condensed. But the **I AM** too is a solidified illusion of **CONSCIOUSNESS**, which is **NOTHING** only.

PRESENCE IS PART OF THE I AM. THE I AM CONCEPT IS PRESENCE THAT I-AM-NESS PRESENCE SHOULD NOT BE THERE. THE NON-I AMNESS ONLY CAN MEET THE NOTHINGNESS

NISARGADATTA MAHARAJ

To realize the **NOTHINGNESS**, "one" might first trace everything back to the non-verbal **I AM** and stay there until the **NOTHING** or pure **CONSCIOUSNESS** is revealed. Many confuse **THAT** with the **I AM**'s presence or silence. This is incorrect. The **I AMNESS,** as the primal illusion, has presence, and it is this presence which seductively conceals its illusionary nature - that it is made of **NOTHINGNESS**.

THE I AM IS THE CLOAK WHICH VEILS THE NOTHINGNESS

NISARGADATTA MAHARAJ

Presence is part of the **I AM** lens. In this way, presence is part of, or is a by-product of, the **I AM**. This **I AMNESS** with its presence is the seductive vehicle of **CONSCIOUSNESS**, which reflects and creates the "you character," and all that the "you" calls itself, and "convinces" it into believing the concept of being.

THE KNOWLEDGE I AM HAS COME OUT OF THE PRIOR STATE WHERE THERE WAS NO CONSCIOUSNESS

NISARGADATTA MAHARAJ

From **NOTHING** the **I AM** appears. This **NOTHING** is prior to the **I AM** and it is where there was no **CONSCIOUS-NESS,** because even the concept of **CONSCIOUSNESS** is part of the *mirage*.

It is for this reason that if we stay with the **I AM**, the **EMPTINESS** prior to **CONSCIOUSNESS** is revealed. In Quantum Psychology, we call this the **NOT-I-I**.

ENQUIRY INTO THE NOT-I-I
APPERCEIVING THE EMPTINESS BEYOND I AM

Enquiry Step I   Without using your thoughts, memory, emotions, associations, perceptions, attention or intentions, notice the no-state state or stateless state of the non-verbal **I AM.**

Enquiry Step II   Allow your awareness to move or expand backward or outward, or to fall backward and notice the **BIG EMP-TINESS.**

When the I AM is stayed with
the Not-I-I is revealed

Stephen Wolinsky

THE NOT-I-I

Question: You seem to indicate that the **NOT-I-I** is **WITNESS-ING** the **EMPTINESS**.

Stephen: Yes, but I don't want you to mis-understand. **WIT-NESSING** of the **EMPTINESS** or pure awareness, or the arising and subsiding of an observer-observed, either happens or it doesn't. But whether the **WIT-NESS** happens or not - it is not you. It is an occurrence within **UNDIFFERENTIATED CON-SCIOUSNESS** or **THAT ONE SUBSTANCE**.

Question: But you imply that doing or dismantling identities leads to **WITNESSING**.

Stephen: No, at first there is an *appearance*, as if there is a "you" doing I-dentity work. At some point "you" get that the work is just happening spontaneously and you are not the work*er* or work*ee*.

Question: But this process does help to discover **WHO YOU ARE**.

Stephen: No, it is like saying a man eating at a Chinese restaurant five miles from here helps you to discover **WHO YOU ARE** - obviously he doesn't. You will never discover who you are, because, upon investigation or enquiry, the "I" or—this is "me"—is no more. *The great illusion in this WHO AM I is that you will discover who you are.* You won't because there is no you. In other words, *you* disappear upon investigation. *There is no "I" that you are.*

Question: Then, why do the identity work?

Stephen: "You" do not do the work. It happens or not - it has nothing to do with you. At first a person is attracted to Quantum Psychology or **WHO AM I**, imagining that they will be free, learn psychological techniques, process identities, handle their life. The process makes sense to an individual mind. It is reasonable. But this is only in the beginning—later, you will see it has nothing to do with anything. Quantum Psychology got your attention away from focusing, identifying, and fusing with the **I AM**'s reflection and to focus on and be the **I AM**. Once this is accomplished, you soon realize there is no False Core-False Self, that it is a reflection, an appearance, and that whether there is or is not an identity or problem or not, *has nothing whatsoever to do with you*. Soon, **WITNESSING** occurs—but even the **WITNESS** is a phenomena which appears to arise in **THAT**, but it too *has nothing to do with with anything*. This "you" believes that all this has something to do with "you" because that's what the "you" wants to believe. But **THERE IS NO-YOU**. There is no doer, everything just happens and the idea of a doer is the illusion.

To paraphrase Nisargadatta Maharaj, *When a sperm and an egg came together, it made this body. There was no choice or volition involved. It happened on its own. Now someone wants to take credit for the body-mind-personality. It all just happened - and the idea that I did this or that is the illusion.*

WITNESSING is a phenomena. Like an identity, it occurs or it doesn't. "When" the **WITNESS** realizes it is made of the same substance as everything else - it disappears or evaporates. But whether it disappears or remains, or whether there is identification or not with an identity – they have no effect on **THAT**.

THE SPACE IS THE EYEGLASS OF THE "I AM"

NISARGADATTA MAHARAJ
(Pg. 23, Seeds of CONSCIOUSNESS)

ENQUIRY PROCESS:

Enquiry Step I   *Apperceive* the **I AM** and its projected reflection as being made of the same **CONSCIOUSNESS**.

Enquiry Step II   Stay in the stateless state of **I AM**.

Enquiry Step III   Allow your awareness to move or
                       fall backward or outward and no-
                       tice the **BIG EMPTINESS**.

Enquiry Step IV   *Apperceive the EMPTINESS Be-
                       yond the I AM and its reflections.*

Enquiry Step V   Allow the awar*er* and the **EMP-
                       TINESS** to be the same sub-
                       stance.

YOU MUST SPONTANEOUSLY FEEL
THE SUPERFICIALITY OF "I AMNESS"

NISARGADATTA MAHARAJ

(Pg. 36, Seeds Of CONSCIOUSNESS)

Once you stay in **I AM**, the identification with its projected images dissolves, and soon too does the **I AM**. Without an **I
AM** vehicle for **CONSCIOUSNESS**, all projected images and
characters on the screen are gone. The **CONSCIOUSNESS** through
the **I AM** is like a movie projector projecting out its images, which
then imagine they are alive, real, are *born* and will *die* and then be
reborn. But when the **I AM** is *apperceived* as the same substance
(**CONSCIOUSNESS**) as its reflection, both disappear and the
EMPTINESS is revealed. When the **EMPTINESS** and the awar*er*
are *apperceived* as the same **EMPTINESS**, there is No-Me
Samadhi.

THE KNOWLEDGE I AM IS NOT LEFT
AFTER DEATH, SO HOW CAN THERE BE ANY
QUESTIONS OF FURTHER BIRTHS? THE FACT IS
THAT NOTHING IS BORN, THERE IS NO WORLD.
THE WORLD APPEARS BUT IT IS NOT THERE.
THERE IS NO SUCH THING AS ENLIGHTENMENT.

THESE CONCEPTS—REINCARNATION, ETC.
ARE MEANT FOR THE IGNORANT.

NISARGADATTA MAHARAJ
(Pg. 200 The Ultimate Medicine)

Two

PSYCHOLOGY

. . . .

PERSONALITY IS A MIS-TAKEN IDENTITY

NISARGADATTA MAHARAJ

PSYCHOLOGY

Let us begin this discussion by dividing psychology into two separate areas. First, what "you" call your *personal psychology*; and, second, the *Field of Psychology*, which proposes healing, transforming, or fixing a wounded self, creating a new self, resolving the past self, or what you call "you" and "your" personal psychology.

PERSONAL PSYCHOLOGY

The explanations, justifications, stories, reasons, causes and effects - in short, all you call "you" and "your" psychology - arises out of, and is ultimately a projected reflection of **CONSCIOUSNESS** through the **I AM**. Once this psychology which justifies, re-enforces, and proves **I AM**, is believed and identified with, the illusion of a "you" takes hold and gives the appearance of solidness in space-time. From the I-dentification with these abstractions and philosophies called "you", psychology emerges which drives us deeper and deeper into the trap of believing our mind, and further away from the pure **I AM** or the **CONSCIOUSNESS** which the **I AM** is made of prior to its projected-reflections.

Nisargadatta never spoke directly to or about the field of psychology. He never made reference in any direct or indirect way about classical psychology, its philosophy, thought or techniques. Rather, he focused on the **I AM**, and what stood in the way of its *realization*. Nisargadatta Maharaj himself was the embodiment of the **INNER SELF-I AM** and beyond it - **THAT**. It is with this understanding that we again repeat his words.

YOGA IS THE WORK ON THE INNER SELF ON THE OUTER SELF

NISARGADATTA MAHARAJ

In this way, Nisargadatta Maharaj never placed a *cause*, or *reason* (as does your personal psychology, as well as the field of psychology) as to *why* one does this or that. He undersood that looking for causes, meanings, or reasons, were attempts by the nervous system to survive and to gain control. He *realized* and taught that everything happens as it happens with no reasons or causes. He knew, in this way, not to fall for the illusion of **CONSCIOUSNESS** through the **I AM**'s reflection→identification.

In order to get us to let go of this seductive psychology, he smashed, through confrontation, the personal and psychological lenses and frames of reference which were the reflected projection of **CONSCIOUSNESS** through the **I AM,** and which, through identification, keep us *split-off* from **I AM**.

Nisargadatta Maharaj knew that the person "you" call "yourself" intermediately could be said to be a reflection of **I AM,** but that ultimately it was just a *mirage made of CONSCIOUSNESS*.

THE MIRROR REFLECTS THE IMAGE BUT THE IMAGE DOES NOT IMPROVE THE MIRROR. YOU ARE NEITHER THE MIRROR NOR THE IMAGE.

NISARGADATTA MAHARAJ
(Pg. 330, I Am That)

"YOU ARE NOT A PERSON."

NISARGADATTA MAHARAJ

Furthermore, *he never tried to get us to improve* the person *realizing* the person was also an illusion. He never tried to change a person or suggested a personal healing process as does the field of psychology. Neither did he suggest or denounce desires as bad, habits as something to be gotten rid of, nor emotions, such as anger, or fear as signs of some type of dysfunction, a sin or a vice. And he never, on the other side, exhalted love, compassion, forgiveness, or bliss as virtues, or something to develop or strive for. He always knew the person was a *mirage* (see Chapter XII), an image made of solidified light we could call **CONSCIOUSNESS**. Simply put, why try to change what is not you.

NOTHING YOU DO WILL CHANGE YOU, FOR YOU NEED NO CHANGE. YOU MAY CHANGE YOUR MIND OR BODY, BUT IT IS ALWAYS SOMETHING EXTERNAL TO YOU THAT HAS CHANGED. NOT YOURSELF.

NISARGADATTA MAHARAJ
(Pg. 520, I AM THAT)

In short, you can change an image, which is all you think you are, *but it is not you.*

Nisargadatta Maharaj was not a psychologist or a body-worker interested in function. His interest and stress lay entirely on forcing you through the confrontation of who you thought you were (i.e., identities) by bringing everything into awareness. In this way,. the **I AM** reflection (which was made of **CONSCIOUS-NESS**) arose and its inherent falseness could be viewed. And also in this way, it would disappear upon investigation, as the pure **I AM** and the **CONSCIOUSNESS** the **I AM** was made of, were realized.

Along the same vein, a friend of mine once told me that Bagawan Nityananda appeared to him in a vision and said,

"Give me your Ego"

In this way Nisargadatta Maharaj confronted our I-dentities "wanting" them to evaporate, because he said,

YOU CANNOT LET GO OF SOMETHING
UNTIL YOU KNOW WHAT IT IS.

NISARGADATTA MAHARAJ
(NISARGA MEANS NATURAL)

THE STYLE

In fact, if I were to describe **NISARGA YOGA** it could easily summed up as follows:

1) **CONFRONTATION** to bring up the concepts of oneself, which hold the primal concept **I AM** solid;
2) **ENQUIRY** into the concepts or **I AM**'s reflection;
3) The *disappearance (evaporation) / discarding* of concepts upon **INVESTIGATION** and enquiry;
4) **ABIDANCE** in the **I AM**;
5) And the Evaporation of **I AM** and *apperception* of the **CONSCIOUSNESS** and the **NOTHINGNESS** Beyond.

MOST OF YOUR EXPERIENCES
ARE UNCONSCIOUS. . . .
BECOME AWARE OF THE UNCONSCIOUS. . . .
YOU CANNOT LET GO OF SOMETHING
UNTIL YOU KNOW WHAT IT IS.

NISARGADATTA MAHARAJ
(PG. 406, I AM THAT)

Nisargadatta Maharaj confronted the unconscious so that it could arise into awareness, be investigated, and then discarded. It was by discarding the images of the unconscious through confrontation→ enquiry→ investigating all→ disappearance→ **I AM**→ **CONSCIOUSNESS**→ **NOTHINGNESS.**

Meher Baba used to say the ego is like an iceberg. Ninety percent of it is underwater. Through confrontation and enquiry, the iceberg arises into the light of awareness so that it melts, dissolves, and evaporates.

In this way, quite *spontaneously*, with no *inner considering* or *pre-meditation* Nisargadatta Maharaj spontaneously attacked and liberated the conceptual framework of who "one" "thought" "one" was and was holding onto.

Two points need to be clarified: 1) This was not planned. He did not think, "Oh, this person needs this or that." Rather, it just happened. The spontaneity of Nisargadatta Maharaj often led to a feeling of being shocked or shattered. The first time Nisargadatta Maharaj confronted me I felt like my body had burst into flames. To repeat:

THIS IS A PLACE WHERE
THE INTELLECT GETS ANNIHILATED.

NISARGADATTA MAHARAJ

(PG. 46, ABSOLUTE AND THE ABSOLUTE)

Nisargadatta Maharaj seemed to go where your most deeply-seated concepts were rooted. This, on the receiving end, was not always a pleasant process because "I", like everyone else, had organized a life around ideas, and frames of reference which were not "me".

The pain was that "I" did not know that these were concepts, ideas, and frames of reference, that they were not me. "I" thought they were "me" and that if they died, so would the "I" "I" thought I was. This was terrifically painful for "me".

Second, he would confront and bring-up everything for enquiry and scrutiny. No concept was sacred no societal rules of nice, no context of "safety", no rapport building - in short, no Western psychological support games where used. From the *outside*, this could be seen as cruel, mean, and even abusive. For me, "I" somehow knew its purpose and so there was total surrender to the process. From the *inside*, years later, "I" realized that all of the above-mentioned therapeutic techniques were games that therapists created to ensure an on-going relationship, which was not always for the benefit of the student or client - but oftentimes was for the benefit of therapists or teachers whose needs of worth, connection, adequacy, love, power, etc., need to be filled.

In the short run, this way of having a mirror held in front of you, showing you your darkest or deepest concepts, can be quite painful; however in the long run it is liberating.

This might explain what we used to say about the difference between old-timers and new-comers around a guru. The new comers want to *be close* - the old timers *stay away*. Why? Because the shattering and shock can be and is overwhelming.

This is why Nisargadatta never encouraged people to come; and, in fact, he actually discouraged people and even threw many out. He threw me out on the eighth day. I returned many times, however, and sometimes he let me stay, sometimes not. But I could not resist him or his words, which were on one level painful, and on another, ecstatic and liberating.

Nisargadatta did not care about the delivery of the message, or even how the information would be received. Any concept was fair-game and if you came to see him, as "I" did, he assumed that you understood that there were no holds barred in his (the **INNER SELF**'s) work on the outer self.

In this way, there was no 20th century age-regressed reflective listening or unconditional positive regard. (My psychology mentor, Dr. Eric Marcus, used to call unconditional positive regard, "unconditional positive disregard.") In fact, if you think about it, *regard for what*? You suffer because you give and have so much regard for the I-dentities, ideas, concepts and images which *are not you*. To "get over" having so much regard for what is not you, you have to stop falling in love with the ideas, images, and the reflected character of the **I AM CONSCIOUSNESS**.

For Nisargadatta Maharaj, you were not a person or an idea. A person was a projected image of **CONSCIOUSNESS** through the **I AM**, a bio-chemical reaction; and once these concepts and unquestioned images were peeled back and dismantled, the **I AM** could be seen-known-experienced and, ultimately, *apperceived* and gone beyond.

WHILE LOOKING AT THE MIND YOU CANNOT GO BEYOND IT. TO GO BEYOND YOU MUST LOOK AWAY FROM THE MIND AND ITS CONTENTS.

NISARGADATTA MAHARAJ
(Pg. 307, I AM THAT)

In order to go beyond "your" psychology, no attention can be given, or attempts made, to change **CONSCIOUSNESS**'s reflection through the **I AM**, i.e., psychology. Stay in the **I AM**, discard personal psychology, and give it no energy or attention. Rather, your attention must be turned around so that the **I AM** can first be *realized* and all else discarded as **NOT-THIS, NOT-THIS**.

CHILDHOOD:
THE CHILD PRINCIPLE

The following is one of the rare statements about childhood made by Nisargadatta Maharaj:

WE ARE TALKING ABOUT THE BEGINNING OF EVERYTHING. IT ALL BEGAN WITH CHILDHOOD. NOW, THAT CHILDHOOD IS ALSO A CONCEPT, AN IDEA. SO, IF YOU UNDERSTAND THAT, YOU TRANSCEND AT ONCE ALL CON-

CEPTS. THAT IS WHY IT IS IMPERATIVE
TO UNDERSTAND CHILDHOOD.

WHAT IS THE FUNCTION OF CHILD-
HOOD? ITS FUNCTION IS FOR YOU TO
KNOW THAT YOU EXIST. THAT IS ALL IT
HAS DONE. PRIOR TO THAT, YOU HAD
NO EXPERIENCE OF THE "I"-CON-
SCIOUSNESS. MY STATEMENT, AND
THAT OF MY GURU, IS THAT CHILD-
HOOD IS A CHEAT, IT IS FALSE. THE
KNOWLEDGE "I AM" ITSELF IS A
CHEAT. WHEN THE BEINGNESS AP-
PEARS, THAT LOVE FOR EXISTENCE IS
THE RESULT OF THE PRIMARY ILLU-
SION, THAT MAYA. ONCE YOU COME
TO KNOW THAT YOU EXIST, YOU FEEL
LIKE ENDURING ETERNALLY. YOU AL-
WAYS WANT TO BE, TO EXIST, TO SUR-
VIVE. AND SO THE STRUGGLE BE-
GINS. ALL BECAUSE OF THAT MAYA.

NISARGADATTA MAHARAJ
(Pg. 60, The Ultimate Medicine)

During the Realization of Separation in childhood (approxi-
mately 5-12 months of age), four things occur: 1) the **I AM** begins
to solidify; 2) the False Core-False Self is formed; 3) the **EMPTI-
NESS** prior to **I AM** is blamed for the infant's separation from
mom; and 4) the child loses identification with **THAT EMPTI-
NESS** and identifies with the body-mind as itself.

THE CHILD PRINCIPLE IS THE FORMATION OF I AM.

NISARGADATTA MAHARAJ

Once the Realization of Separation has occurred in childhood, and the **I AM** begins to form and to solidify body identification and survival become its *SOUL* purpose. This is the *love of existence*, the survival drive. Once this occurs the body joins this **I AM** and False Core-False Self and the body's survival gets wedded to the **I AM**. This must be understood completely, otherwise there will always be an I-dentification with the body and its manufactured facsimiles, the root of which is **I AM**.

WHAT IS THAT CHILDHOOD? WHAT IS THAT CHILD PRINCIPLE? INVESTIGATE THAT. WHEN KRISHNA WAS BORN HE HAD THAT TOUCH OF "I AMNESS" THE SAME GOES FOR YOURSELF. . . . WHEN DID YOU KNOW THAT YOU ARE? IF YOU TRY TO EMPLOY WHATEVER YOU HAVE HEARD, YOU WILL NEVER BE ABLE TO UNDERSTAND THIS. YOU KNOW THAT YOU WERE NOT, BUT NOW YOU KNOW THAT YOU ARE. HOW DID THIS HAPPEN? . . . THIS IS WHAT WE WANT TO DISCOVER.

NISARGADATTA MAHARAJ

(PG. 74-75, THE ULTIMATE MEDICINE)

Because what you call you and *your* "personal psychol-ogy" is a reflection of **CONSCIOUSNESS** through the **I AM** and "further" from **I AM,** its distortions and beliefs that **IT IS** must be investigated and dismantled. Unfortunately, most forms of mod-ern-day therapy focus on the image in the mirror, imagining it is "I" when it is not "I". Thus there is an on-going attempt to improve the image in the mirror (incorrectly imagining it is "I"). In this way, the subject or **I AM** is further forgotten.

It is important to understand that the images and concepts must evaporate in order for the **I AM** to be stabilized. Later, the **I AM** dissolves as well.

AS SALT DISSOLVES IN WATER SO DOES EVERYTHING DISSOLVE IN PURE BEING. WISDOM IS ETERNALLY NEGATING THE UNREAL. TO SEE THE UNREAL IS WISDOM. BEYOND THIS LIES THE INEXPRESSIBLE.

NISARGADATTA MAHARAJ

(Pg. 133, I Am That)

In this way, the projected reflected images of **CONSIOUSNESS I AM** are like salt which dissolves in the ocean of **NOTHINGNESS.** When **I AM** is stabiled, it realizes that all concepts and images are unreal. This is wisdom. Once the **I AM** dissolves, the **VOID** (which, as Nisargadatta Maharaj said, can only be described by what it is not) is revealed.

YOU MUST GRASP THIS CHILD PRINCIPLE. . . . TRACE EVERY ACTION TO ITS SELFISH MOTIVE AND LOOK AT THE MOTIVE INTENTLY UNTIL IT DISSOLVES.

(Pg. 315, I Am That)

With the child principle, the formation of the **I AM** and the False Core-False Self, is solidified. Soon all mental concepts and knowledge, i.e., your individual psychology is formed to justify, re-enforce and ensure its survival. Trace all of your thoughts, feelings, emotions, associations, perceptions, fantasies, intentions, etc., back to the False Core-False Self and then to the non-verbal **I AM**. This takes "you" prior to **I AM**, to the **CONSCIOUSNESS** the **I AM** is made of.

To discover **WHO YOU ARE**, this Realization of Separation and the emergence of **I AM** must be investigated for what it is. Do not give life or attention to the made-up stories of one's "personal" psychology, which follows the **I AM**. Stay in the **I AM**, discover how it works, *trace* everything back to **I AM,** and then, it will dissolve as does the illusion of everything upon investigation.

ACTION

I DO NOT REMEMBER SOMETHING FROM THE PAST AND THEN ACT; ALL ACTIONS ARE IN THE NOW.

NISARGADATTA MAHARAJ

(Pg. 21, Consciousness and the Absolute)

Most people use inner considering or even shift or censure their words to match what they imagine the environment wants. They look "functional"; however these shifting words, phrases, and emotions, in an attempt to get what you want, are subtlely based on survival. This re-enforces the survival of the "I", and worse yet, it gobbles up awareness and makes you believe in the reflection of **CONSCIOUSNESS** through the **I AM**.

INVESTIGATE AND DISCARD

WHATEVER KNOWLEDGE YOU HAVE IS HEARSAY. EVERYTHING YOU KNOW ABOUT YOURSELF CAME FROM OUTSIDE–THEREFORE DISCARD IT.

NISARGADATTA MAHARAJ

All knowledge or information is only hearsay, it is an *opinion* of others - once investigated, it disappears.

EVERYTHING DISAPPEARS UPON INVESTIGATION

NISARGADATTA MAHARAJ

The knowledge called psychology is based on abstractions and presuppositions. Therefore, its solution, called psychotherapy, is a solution based on a false conclusion and hence more false than hearsay.

SORTING OUT AND DISCARDING ARE ABSOLUTELY NECESSARY

NISARGADATTA MAHARAJ

Staying in the **I AM** and discarding everything represents the sanskrit **NETI-NETI-, NOT THIS, NOT THIS**, and it is the process whereby the **I AM** gets stabilized.

BEYOND THE OBSERVER

ULTIMATELY, EVEN THE OBSERVER YOU ARE NOT

NISARGADATTA MAHARAJ

Going beyond the observer and its observed object is pivotal to stabilizing in **I AM**.

PROCESS:

Enquiry into the nature of the observer-observed;

Step I: Notice a thought.

Step II: Be the observer of the thought.

Step III: Notice what occurs when "I" ask, "What observer is observing that?"

People go into the blank no-state state of **I AM**, because the illusion that there is one observer is dispelled as the observer-observed dyad evaporates. There are an infinite number of observers. With each experience a different observer arises and subsides. The illusion of one observer naturally evaporates as the **I AM** is stabilized.

MENTAL PURIFICATION
AND DESTRUCTION

SEE THE UNREAL AS UNREAL AND DISCARD IT. IT IS THE DISCARDING THE FALSE WHICH OPENS THE WAY TO THE TRUE. . . THIS WORK OF MENTAL SELF-PURIFICATION, THE CLEANSING OF THE PSYCHE, IS ESSENTIAL

NISARGADATTA MAHARAJ
(Pg. 315, I Am That)

Cleansing here means investigation which leads one to enquire into concepts one has about "oneself," *the number one concept being I AM.* This investigtion→ confrontation→ enquiry→evaporation brings concepts into awareness and "on-screen." Investigation and confrontation lead to enquiry, and through enquiry comes evaporation, and the realization of the illusionary power of the concepts. Discard them until the discard*er* too is no longer.

The root is **I AM**. Nisargadatta continually points us to **I AM** as the gateway or portal which will lead us to its source - **CONSCIOUSNESS**

IT IS SEEING THE FALSE AS FALSE AND REJECTING IT . . . SORTING OUT AND DISCARDING ARE ABSOLUTELY NECESSARY. EVERYTHING MUST BE SCRUTINIZED AND THE UNNECESSARY RUTHLESSLY DESTROYED. BELIEVE ME, THERE CANNOT BE TOO MUCH DESTRUCTION.

NISARGADATTA MAHARAJ
(Pg. 84, I AM THAT)

THE CONCEPT OF BONDAGE

Conclusions and concepts that are held bind only the you you think you are. They can never bind *you*, because you are **THAT**.

YOUR CONCLUSIONS BIND NOBODY BUT YOU. . . . YOUR OWN CONCEPTS WILL ONLY SERVE AS AN INSTRUMENT OF BONDAGE

NISARGADATTA MAHARAJ
(PG. 83, CONSCIOUSNESS AND THE ABSOLUTE)

The basic principle is that whatever you think you are, you are not. For this reason, as the *Siva Sutras* say, "Knowledge is bondage". Why? Because all knowledge is - and can only be - conceptual. A concept is only a projected reflection of **CONSCIOUSNESS** solidified through the **I AM** concept, and hence it can only lead to more concepts and abstractions, and even further away from its source which is **CONSCIOUSNESS, the I AM** and its **EVAPORATION**.

THE COLLECTIVE AND UNDIFFERENTIATED CONSCIOUSNESS OR EMPTINESS

THE I AM COMES FROM THE COLLECTIVE

NISARGADATTA MAHARAJ

YOUR THOUGHTS ABOUT INDIVIDUALITY ARE REALLY NOT YOUR THOUGHTS; THEY ARE COLLECTIVE THOUGHTS. YOU THINK YOU ARE THE ONE WHO HAS THE THOUGHTS; IN FACT THOUGHTS ARISE IN CONSCIOUSNESS

NISARGADATTA MAHARAJ
(Pg. 9, Consciousness and the Absolute)

Thoughts, according to Nisargadatta, are not yours. Rather, the thinker of the thought is contained within the thought itself. Furthermore, the thinker of the thought is part of the thought itself, and both are made of or are condensations of **UNDIFFERENTIATED CONSCIOUSNESS** or **EMPTINESS**. They are not yours nor do they belong to a "you". The "you" or "I" appears with each thought as each thought arises. The process is almost instantaneous.

THE "I" APPEARS OUT OF NOTHING, AND GOES BACK INTO NOTHING.

NISARGADATTA MAHARAJ

ENQUIRY INTO THE THINKER

In order to *apperceive* the nature of the thinker and the thought, an enquiry is provided below:

ENQUIRY

Step I   Notice a thought.

Step II   Notice that the think*er* of the thought is contained within the thought itself.

ENQUIRY

Step I   Notice a thought.

Step II   Notice what occurs when "I" say, "What think*er* is thinking that?" Notice the blankness of the non-verbal **I AM** as the think*er* of the thought and that thought itself disappears upon investigation.

In this way, the "one" who claims these are *my* thoughts does not understand that the claim*er* or concept of an owner of the thought is part of the thought itself. *All thoughts occur in the context of, and contain, I AM - YOU ARE, and they are collective in nature.* It is an illusion that there is a separate think*er* which thinks thoughts which belong to a separate you.

PSYCHOLOGY'S LAST STAND

WE ARE SLAVES TO WHAT WE DO NOT KNOW, OF WHAT WE KNOW WE ARE MASTERS. . . . THE UNCONSCIOUS DISSOLVES WHEN BROUGHT INTO THE CONSCIOUS.

NISARGADATTA MAHARAJ
(Pg. 13, I Am That)

Hence we see "some" possibility, hope or last stand for psychology. *Not an analysis based on presumptions*, which tries to change or heal a "personal psychology story" but on just "looking" with awareness at what is there, realizing it is not you, and discarding it.

WHAT YOU SEE AS FAKE DISSOLVES. IT IS THE VERY NATURE OF ILLUSION TO DISSOLVE ON INVESTIGATION.

(Pg. 455, I Am That)

This is the process, investigate-confront→ bringing up into awareness→ enquire→ confronting the concept→ discarding→ abidance in yourself—the **I AM**.

DISCARD ALL YOU ARE NOT AND GO EVEN DEEPER. JUST AS A MAN DIGGING A WELL DISCARDS WHAT IS NOT WATER, DISCARD UNTIL NOTHING IS LEFT. . . . GIVE-UP THE TENDENCY TO DEFINE YOURSELF

NISARGADATTA MAHARAJ
(Pg. 320, I AM THAT)

Unlike the field of psychology which attempts to define, diagnose, heal, transform, or change thoughts, images, emotions, memory, associations, perceptions, attention or intentions, Nisargadatta Maharaj asks us to discard all and stay in **I AM**; *without using* thoughts, memory, emotions, associations, perceptions, attention, or intentions.

AFTER THE DISAPPEARANCE OF EVERYTHING, WHATEVER REMAINS, THAT YOU ARE; NETI-NETI

NISARGADATTA MAHARAJ

(PG. 84, THE ULTIMATE MEDICINE)

Question: Why does Quantum Psychology, as well as the Patanjali's Yoga Sutras, talk of polarities.

Stephen: According to Nisargadatta Maharaj, everything has an opposite.

"AT THE RELATIVE LEVEL EVERYTHING HAS AN INTER-RELATED COUNTERPART, LIKE LIGHT AND DARKNESS, GOOD AND BAD. EACH NEGATES THE OTHER."

NISARGADATTA MAHARAJ

Question: I want to be here now.

"BEING HERE NOW MEANS BEING IN THE ABSENCE OF SPACE-TIME"

NISARGADATTA MAHARAJ

In this incredible statement, even the idea of having a beginning is *NOW*, even memories of the past are *NOW*, even if you did this to me six months ago it is occurring now. The coming and going of different moments each only appears *NOW.*

EACH MOMENT APPEARS OUT OF NOTHING AND DISAPPEARS INTO NOTHING

NISARGADATTA MAHARAJ

Developing communication skills, getting what you want, has *nothing* to do with finding out **WHO YOU ARE**.

In fact, wanting to find out **WHO YOU ARE** has nothing to do with finding **WHO YOU ARE**.

Question: It seems that what you're saying contradicts what you have said in the past. Doesn't giving up I-dentities etc., help to liberate awareness and free you?

Stephen: You are confusing awareness and observation. Observation and the observer are part of the observed. Awareness is beyond the observer-observed dyad. Observation is part of the illusion and trap. Observation is part of the Observer-**I AM** *mirage.* Anything, like getting to know yourself, observing, being in touch with feelings, etc., etc., etc. - and I mean anything - *can be* a dangerously seductive trap because it still holds a subtle pre-supposition that somehow you will "work through it and then be happy", in bliss, etc. It's bullshit. There is an illusion among

people, particularly psychology fans, that being
"healthy" means always doing and saying the "right"
thing, not getting angry, being compassionate, etc.
People imagine that, in short, psychological health,
which is only part of some standard or definition,
has something to do with finding out **WHO YOU
ARE**. It doesn't. The root of the problem is the **I
AM**. When there is no **I AM**, there is no personal
psychology, problem, doer, doing, or spirituality.

Spirituality is only a concept of the **I AM** and is part of the
mirage of **CONSCIOUSNESS**. To repeat:

NOTHING YOU DO WILL CHANGE YOU, FOR YOU NEED NO CHANGE. YOU MAY CHANGE YOUR MIND OR BODY, BUT IT IS ALWAYS SOMETHING EXTERNAL TO YOU THAT CHANGES, NOT YOURSELF.

NISARGADATTA MAHARAJ
(Pg. 520, I Am That)

Question: But you have said that uncooked seeds pull aware-
                 ness out of the **VOID**.

Stephen: Yes, and I was answering like that for *beginners* to
                 begin to see that it is all part of the **I AM DREAM-
                 MIRAGE**.

For example, in order to go beyond the crucial concept of
location we might enquire: "What concept does the concept **I AM**
have about the concept of location?" Well this question is dependent on four concepts: 1) It pre-supposes that there is an **I AM**; 2)
that there are concepts; 3) that there is location; and 4) subtly, that
if you do this process you will get there when there *is no there*. The

purpose of these processes is to *cut* ideas, concepts, and images of **I AM** at their roots so that stabilization in **I AM** is natural.

PRIOR TO: I AM

I HAVE PUT AN AX AT THE VERY ROOT; THERE IS NO QUESTION OF SPROUTING. WHATEVER MY STATE WAS PRIOR TO THE CHILD IS MY STATE.

NISARGADATTA MAHARAJ
(Pg. 190, Seeds Of Consciousness)

THE FALSE SELF AND SPIRITUAL PRACTICE

Question: But the **VOID** is there?

Stephen: Ultimately, there is no **VOID**. The experience of a **VOID** or **VOID** universes is dependent upon a know*er* or **CONSCIOUSNESS**, in short an experienc*er*. Since these are non-existent, there can be no **VOID** because it requires an "I" there to say, "This is the **VOID**." Even the knowledge of the **VOID** requires a know*er*. Every know*er* contains only certain specific knowledge and knowing - no knower, no experienc*er* no known, experience or **VOID**. In short, no **I AM**, no personal psychology, and No-You.

Question: But can't psycho-spiritual practice help to get beyond the knower-known?

Stephen: Most psycho-spiritual practice is done by a False
              Self trying to survive what Maharaj calls its *love of
              existence*. If this is true, then psycho-spiritual prac-
              tice oftentimes can re-enforce the False Core-False
              Self since the False Self is trying to get something
              or it imagines it will find out who it is, when it is
              NOT. There is no way out of this dilemma, other
              than to *apperceive* through it, to stay in the **I AM**
              and *BE*.

THE FALSE SELF
WANTS TO CONTINUE PLEASANTLY.

NISARGADATTA MAHARAJ
(Pg. 298, I Am That)

A major obstacle to this is that False Self is determined to
look for the positive reframe. This reframing not only re-enforces
the False Core, *and that it is*, but it keeps one away from investigating the child principle, the shock of the Realization of Separation and the formation of **I AM**.

Question: But isn't giving support to others a spiritual quality?

Stephen: To begin with, giving support or safety is an attempt
              by the False Self to give "safety" or "support" to
              another so that they can then feel safe. "I" knew a
              therapist who obsessively gave what she called sup-
              port to everyone. However, in reality, it was the way
              she could feel safe. In other words, her False Self
              gave support (safety) to others, so that she would
              feel safe and supported, and did not have to feel her
              feelings of "I am not safe or supported," thus re-
              enforcing the whole process.

Moreover, developing what is commonly called "spiritual" qualities is bullshit. Spiritual qualities for whom? A non-existent self? There is no such thing as a spiritual quality. Because the **NOTHING**, and even the **I AM**, have no qualities or attributes; *no frames of reference, no references to frame.*

Question: But when the False Core-False Self is gone, doesn't behavior change?

Stephen: *Maybe.* The outward behavior may still remain the same - but there is *NO* subjective experience of it or even caring about it. Even better said, there is no subjective experience—it is totally **EMPTY**.

PSYCHOLOGY'S MISNOMER: THE CONCEPT OF CHANGE

Question: Quantum Psychology seems to say psychology is bullshit - why?

Stephen: Because it attempts to heal the problem of a non-existent self, a self which is like a reflection in a mirror. It continues to re-enforce the process by try-ing to make the **I AM**'s reflection better.

DON'T TRY TO REFORM YOURSELF, JUST SEE THE FUTILITY OF ALL CHANGE, SEE THE VERY IDEA OF CHANGING AS FALSE.

NISARGADATTA MAHARAJ
(Pg. 521, I AM THAT)

Any attempt to turn yourself into a better person is ridicu-lous, it is like a shadow or *mirage* trying to be a better *mirage*.

What psychology does not understand is that the person, the "I", and its psychology are all made of the same **CONSCIOUSNESS,** which appears as different substances through the **I AM.** The concept of change lies at the root of the deception of the **CONSCIOUSNESS** through the **I AM**'s identification, all of which arises out of the **CONDENSED CONSCIOUSNESS** called **I AM** (see Chapter One, **I AM**). To discover **WHO YOU ARE**, the chang*er* and the concept of change too must be seen intermittently as a reflection of the **I AM,** and ultimately as **CONSCIOUSNESS.**

Question: Yet you use psychology in volumes I and II of *The Way of The Human* to explain behavior.

Stephen: To offer a *story* as to why. The purpose behind this is to get psychology fans to turn inward. To get psychology and spiritual buffs to confront and question, and turn psychology and spirituality on itself, to *question and investigate* itself - its purpose, motives, and underlying pre-suppositions. *It uses a thorn* (psychology and spirituality) *to remove a thorn* (psychology and spirituality). It was an attempt to use reason to get people to question psychology and spirituality so that they can see it is laden with pre-suppositions, which are not true, and to answer the question why "people", after ten, twenty or even thirty years of therapy or spiritual practice, are still in pain.

Question: Well, it really pissed people off.

Stephen: I'm sure it did. When pure reason, or *sattva*, does not work, and you are investigating and confronting *tomas* (interia), force *raja* is sometimes necessary. It is not easy to investigate and confront your delusions - *most of psychology and spirituality is delusional, and their concepts are unquestioned and held as sacred.* To illustrate how many pre-suppositions remain unquestioned and resisted among scientists, look at what happened around the planet Jupiter. For centuries, scientists could not understand why this spot on Jupiter moved. It drove scientists crazy. How could a spot on a solid planet move? Then in the 1970s, they discovered that Jupiter was not solid, but a gas so the spot naturally moves. In the same way, *our perceptions of a solid "I" and solid world are untrue presuppositions.* The intense belief to "see" the world and "I" as solid when they are not drives people crazy.

Question: How do you know if you are deluding yourself?

Stephen: Pain will let you know.

Question: But people are pissed at you!

Stephen: Of course, it is easier to try to discredit the messenger than *confront the message.* Remember the False Core-False Self and all its philosophies and structures are created by the nervous system for survival. Therefore, there is a natural fight-flight-freeze response. If they are angry at me, *they don't have to look at themselves or the message.* When people try to fight the messenger or the message, they resist taking-in the message. This keeps the message in place, and literally, over time, the message destroys who the person imagines themselves to be, and everything they imagine is important. Believe me, it is not a pleasant process. So, ultimately, they have to look at themselves; or suffer.

When I was confronted by Nisargadatta Maharaj, "I" could not stand up straight for *two years* until "I" finally got through it, and there was no resistance on "my" part. If you resist and fight the process, it can mean a lifetime of pain. There seems to be a tendency to project the source of your pain or problem on another, and then create a philosophy to justify and blame the other rather than to look at your concepts. Actually, at one level, we could say that, in the brain stem, there is a very primitive tendency, which when it gets triggered, it tries to kill what is perceived as the source of its pain. This can be done through actually killing, such as what was done by the Nazis, or in Africa or in Bosnia or Kosovo. When killing cannot be done, then psychological killing through psychological diagnosis is the more "civilized" or socially acceptable approach. Simply put, it is easier to make your problem, concepts, and pain, another's problem.

THIS IS ALL PART OF THE DEMOLITION PROCESS. TO START WITH YOU MUST BE COMPLETELY DISMANTLED...BEFORE THE SEED IS PLANTED, THE GROUND MUST BE CULTIVATED AND FERTILIZED. ONLY AFTER PLOWING THE GROUND AND PLANTING THE SEED WILL THE SPROUTING TAKE PLACE. THIS DEMOLISHING PROCESS IS NECESSARY, WHAT REMAINS IS ONLY CONSCIOUSNESS.

NISARGADATTA MAHARAJ
(Pg. 82, Seeds Of Consciousness)

Question: You seem to really put down psychology.

Stephen: There is no PAST. Even the idea of an experience of the past is only happening NOW. In the field of psychology mistakenly theorizes a past causing a present. *The field of psychology does not understand, that no matter what happens, it happens in this moment of space-time. Psychology does not understand that the present contains the past with a fantasized cause which are all one unit which arise and subside together NOW!!* The philosophy as to why I am the way I am *now* BECAUSE of what happened in the past is absurd. Psychology does not understand that the past yielding present are *False causes* and are only attempts to justify and control outcomes. Although they make sense, they are not true. Once we believe in **FALSE CAUSES**, then innumerable **FALSE SOLUTIONS** (therapies and spiritual beliefs) arise, each with minimal results. These philosophies solutions, and therapies are constructions of the nervous system. To repeat again;

THE "NOW" IS, THERE IS ONLY AN ILLUSION OF THE PAST.

Q: I REMEMBER HAVING IT YESTERDAY TOO!

M: THE MEMORY OF YESTERDAY IS NOW ONLY.

Q: BUT SURELY I EXIST IN TIME. I HAVE A PAST AND A FUTURE.

M: THAT IS *NOW* YOU IMAGINE *NOW*.

Q: THERE MUST HAVE BEEN A BEGINNING.

M: *NOW*.

NISARGADATTA MAHARAJ
(Pg, 134, I Am That)

Question: Does Enquiry help?

Stephen: Intermittently yes but bear in mind that enquiry requires an "I" enquir*er* and an enquir*ee*. Both are illusionary and are based on false questions and assumptions. As if an "I" exists, and there is space-time. These phenomenal assumptions are illusionary because they do not exist. There is only **THAT ONE SUBSTANCE**.

Question: But there are patterns?

Stephen: There are no such things as patterns, Patterns, and
                 the idea of a pattern, is an illusion created by the
                 nervous system. It is a survival response, a way to
                 organize the perceived chaos by attributing to events
                 reasons and causes in order to control outcomes. In
                 other words, to survive, the nervous system makes
                 this present time situation appear the same as *that*
                 past time situation; and, in this way, it proceeds the
                 same as it did before in order to survive.

From a psychological point of view, it gives a semblance
of control. If some event happened because I believe (false cause)
this memory or past event, then I further believe that if I handle
this memory or past event then it won't happen again in the future.

**You never put your foot in the
same river twice.**

Heraclitus

There is no pattern. We imagine a pattern, which is part of
the pattern itself. This leads the nervous system into believing that
if we change the pattern, we can change the event yielding control
and survival so **IT** (the unwanted) will not happen again. Psychology reinforces this thus yielding poor, if any results.

Psychology contains within its philosophy a concept that
if "I" can figure out the reason or cause (structure, belief, concept),
I can control what will take place (my state, or state of another). If
I follow this *implicit* philosophy, I believe the reason for what is
lies in the past, and then if I change my belief, then I can change
my present or even future experience.

Some therapies even try to create a future as if an "I" in
the present could change an event for an "I" in the future, or what
will happen in the future (external). This is infantile and grandiose.

In a spiritual context they believe that if you give it up
(bad habit) and do a "spiritual" practice, you will be able to control
realization or bring realization about, which is ridiculous, "as if" *a
you* could control or intend the **VOID** or **THAT**.

Question: In India and Nisargadatta Maharaj teach awareness
               and uncooked Seeds and False Self. Why?.

Stephen: In the beginning, a few pivotal concepts help to or-
               ganize, but you have to go beyond them too. Unfor-
               tunately, psychotherapists, in particular, stop here and
               believe there is a False Core-False Self or an "I" or
               "me" which has them. Soon they try to cure their
               students and themselves from a non-existent struc-
               ture. It is like trying to cure a child of an imaginary
               ghost in the closet. If you open the door and turn on
               the light, you can show the child there is no ghost.
               But if therapists believe in this phantom ghost (from
               the past), they also assume that the ghost has a rea-
               son for being there and that we must heal this imagi-
               nary creature—make it better by transforming it in
               some way. In this way, the therapist has bought into
               and believes the ghost phantom-illusion and soon
               creates a cosmology or philosophy and a technol-
               ogy to explain and try to transform the non-existent
               ghost. The therapist thus re-enforces and justifies his
               theories around this non-existent entity (i.e., a
               memory of mom), thus keeping the illusions even
               more alive. This process only winds up feeding *the
               illusion that there is an "I" which IS.*

      However, if the therapist understands that there is no past,
and that the "I" or self who believes in the past is part of the thought
itself and only **CONSCIOUSNESS** which reflects through the **I
AM,** which it identified had with it as real, then, it disappears. It is
like the old story of the man walking down the street and becoming frightened when he sees a snake. When he realizes it is a rope
- the fear subsides.

Question: So this is why psychology takes so long?

Stephen: Yes, the brainwashing of psychotherapy training
               makes things seem so reasonable, thus it makes it
               difficult for psychotherapists to see their false pre-
               mises. They believe their theories of the past, the

future and cures, etc., not realizing that their memory does not reside in the past. Rather, the images and memory are a reflection of the **I AM**, which arises from **NOTHINGNESS** in **NO-TIME-NOW**, and that psychology with its *after the fact* abstractions and theories, only justify *why* this or that arose. Then, psychotherapists wind-up basing their practice on using these false causes and creating a "how to" as a means to cure them.

Question: Many people I associated with years earlier keep talking to me as if it is then, not now. They don't see me.

Stephen: Yes, the image that arises within "them" of you has nothing to do with you – it is just the image (**I AM** reflection) - don't take it personally because there is no person.

Question: But doesn't Gestalt deal with unfinished business from the past?

Stephen: Only *RIGHT NOW* - what arises is *RIGHT NOW*. This new moment of space time is where **THAT** (Absolute) meets this (**I AM**). This is where the energy is. To repeat again:

THE "NOW" IS, THERE IS ONLY AN ILLUSION OF THE PAST.

Q: I REMEMBER HAVING IT YESTER-
DAY TOO!
M: THE MEMORY OF YESTERDAY IS
NOW ONLY.
Q: BUT SURELY I EXIST IN TIME. I
HAVE A PAST AND A FUTURE.

M: THAT IS *NOW* YOU IMAGINE *NOW.*
Q: THERE MUST HAVE BEEN A BEGIN-
   NING?
M: *NOW.*

NISARGADATTA MAHARAJ
(Pg. 134, I Am That)

In this incredible statement, even the idea of having a beginning is *NOW*, even memory of the past are occurring *NOW*, even
the idea-emotion that you did this to me six months ago is occurring *NOW*. They do not *lie* in a past. They are all only believed
when they come-on screen - right *NOW*. These comings and go-
ings of different moments contain within them the idea of the past,
however, they only appear on screen *NOW*. *There is NO-YOU separate from the experience of you be it a past or a future YOU which
is arising NOW!!*

Question: But therapy can bring about change.

Stephen: Many therapists say to me, "Over the years my cli-
               ents have sure gone through huge transformations."
               Yes, and in over 5, 10 or 20 years, they probably
               would have gone through many life changes any-
               way. You - and all you imagine and experience your-
               self to be – are like a projected reflection in the mir-
               ror. The projected reflection in the mirror is trying
               to change itself. You are the **I AM** subject looking at
               a projected reflection of **CONSCIOUSNESS** and
               then identifying with it. You are *prior* to the reflec-
               tion.

THE I AM AGAIN

Question: But you said the Non-verbal **I AM** has no thoughts, memory, emotions, associations, perceptions, attention or intentions.

Stephen: Yes, the Non-verbal **I AM** has no thoughts, memory, emotions, associations, perceptions, attention or intentions. It is a pointer, a reference point from which your entire universe springs or arises from. When the non-verbal **I AM** dissolves or evaporates, the **I AM** is no longer personal, rather the **I AM** is the entire manifestation of **BEINGNESS**. Once this is realized, through the dissolution of the **I AM** and the realization of **THAT ONE SUBSTANCE**, call it **BEINGNESS, CONSCIOUSNESS** or what have you, this unmanifested **VOID**, or **UNDIFFEREN-TIATED CONSCIOUSNESS—THAT YOU ARE**.

Question: Some Advaita teachers now feel that the **I AM**, or being in the **I AM**, creates an intention and is confusing?

Stephen: They have not understood the difference between **ADVAITA,** *which is verbally unteachable* and **ADVAITA-VEDANTA** *which is teachable*. The stateless state or No-state state is without thoughts, memory, emotions, associations, perceptions, attention or intentions - that is **I AM**.

Question: I don't understand. This seems to be different than earlier statements - The **I AM** is the manifest.

Stephen: The **I AM**, prior to thoughts, memory, emotions, associations, perceptions attention and intentions, is the seed, the lens, the glue which holds your universe together. The universe is a reflection of, and through, the **I AM** - no **I AM**, no universe. This is the meaning of the sanskrit **DRISTI-SHRISTI-VADA** - the world is there only as long as there is a "you" (**I AM**) to perceive it. When the **I AM** touchstone dissolves the entire **manifestation, THAT ONE SUBSTANCE** is **PURE CONSCIOUSNESS,** or pure **BEINGNESS.** The unmanifest **VOID** is just beyond this; and **YOU ARE THAT. APPERCEIVE: DON'T UNDERSTAND.**

Question: I don't understand?

WORDS HEARD OR READ WILL ONLY CREATE IMAGES IN YOUR MIND, BUT YOU ARE NOT MENTAL IMAGES

NISARGADATTA MAHARAJ
(Pg. 510, I Am That)

Stephen: Understanding is the major problem. The process could look like this. First, there is an action. Then, the mind looks for a motivation as to why it did what it did. Then, the mind tries to *understand* the motivation. It then relates this manufactured understanding to what occurred, believing somehow that it will change or could change the consciousness of events that have already taken place.

All motivations and verbal intentions are imagined and manufactured abstractions which arise after the experience or action has already taken place, and only creates a justification for why you did what you did. All this "understanding" does is justify the justification. When it is traced back, it is driven by the nervous systems survival mechanism, i.e., the False Core and a False Cause, so that *later* a remedy is developed so that it (the unwanted) does not happen again.

DON'T TRY TO REFORM YOURSELF.
JUST SEE THE FUTILITY OF CHANGE.
SEE THE VERY IDEA OF CHANGING AS FALSE.

NISARGADATTA MAHARAJ
(PG. 521, I AM THAT)

The concept of change or changing lies *in the mis-understanding that the CONSCIOUSNESS that reflects through the I AM, the I AM, and the reflection, are all made of different substances, not that ONE CONSCIOUSNESS.* To discover **WHO YOU ARE**, the chang*er* too must be seen as a reflection of the **I AM** intermittently, and ultimately as **CONSCIOUSNESS**. Things occur as they occur, the rest is meaningless.

Imagine a room with millions of closed jars. The space in the jars is the non-verbal **I AM**. When the jar is broken, the space fills and becomes the room (unmanifest universe). In this way, the **I AM** is the space in the body which is still and always **THAT ONE SUBSTANCE**; hence, **I AM THAT I AM** space, from which the unmanifest is revealed.

YOU ARE ALWAYS THE SUPREME, BUT YOUR ATTENTION IS FIXED ON THINGS, PHYSICAL OR MENTAL. WHEN YOUR ATTENTION IS OFF ON A THING AND NOT YET FIXED ON ANOTHER,IN THAT INTERVAL YOU ARE PURE BEING.

(PG. 90, I AM THAT)

The space between has been a meditation practice for centuries. The False Self occurs when the **I AM** identifies with **CONSCIOUSNESS**'s projected reflection. The "earliest" phase of **CONSCIOUSNESS**'s projected reflection is the **I AM**. It is through the **I AM** that the False Core-False Self appears.

When the **I AM** is not identified with anything or does not use thoughts, memory, emotions, associations, perceptions, attention or intentions there is pure being.

This is why some of the most famous meditation practices focus on the space between two thoughts, or on the space between two breathes. It is then that you can easily stay in the **I AM**. This is a beginning step. Soon, even the meditat*or* or focus*er* disappears, and then there is only **CONSCIOUSNESS**.

THE SILENCE BEFORE THE WORDS WERE SPOKEN, IS IT DIFFERENT FROM THE SILENCE THAT CAME AFTER

NISARGADATTA MAHARAJ

(Pg. 359, I Am That)

THERAPY'S ILLUSION

Question: You keep saying personal psychology does not exist.

Stephen: The problem is threefold. First, you believe that **YOU ARE** and **I AM**; second, you try to change **CONSCIOUSNESS**'s reflection through the **I AM**, which is not you; and, third, in the process you lose the **I AM** (yourself) at one level. The **I AM** arises out of chemicals coming together, and from that comes what you call "you" and "your personal" psychology. To repeat:

DON'T TRY TO REFORM YOURSELF, JUST SEE THE FUTILITY OF CHANGE; SEE THE VERY IDEA OF CHANGING AS FALSE.

NISARGADATTA MAHARAJ
(Pg. 521, I Am That)

To discover **WHO YOU ARE**, the chang*er* too must be seen as part of the reflection of the **I AM** intermittently and ultimately as **CONSCIOUSNESS**. To repeat yet again;

NOTHING YOU DO WILL CHANGE YOU, FOR YOU NEED NO CHANGE. YOU MAY CHANGE YOUR MIND OR BODY, BUT IT IS ALWAYS SOMETHING EXTERNAL TO YOU THAT CHANGES, NOT YOURSELF.

NISARGADATTA MAHARAJ
(Pg. 521, I Am That)

"Your personal psychology" and psychological solution (therapies) are a reflection of **CONSCIOUSNESS** through the **I AM** (which is also made of **CONSCIOUSNESS**). The reflection believes **IT IS** real and tries to change itself. It isn't that psychology does not exist, it is just that your ideas about the "you" "you" call "yourself" are part of the **REFLECTION**, which, at one level, is a bio-chemical illusion. **YOU ARE** and **I AM** arise and subside in the **NO-TIME NOW**. Contained within them is the illusion of a past, present, future, cause, effect, life, death, and etc. Once the reflection is identified with "it" imagines it is real when it is not.

Question: But some therapies suggest you can create and change the images in your mind. But I keep on feeling like I have problems.

Stephen: The problem is that you identify with the projected reflection of **CONSCIOUSNESS** through the **I AM** and then you look and seek solutions to the problems, be they psychological therapies or spiritual practices with a False Self, all of which is contained within the reflection. You keep on trying to solve the reflection with a False Self reflection solution. The entire process involves the belief in the reflection and the loss of the source of **CONSCIOUSNESS→I AM. It is like a reflection in a mirror imagining it is real and separate from you. To meditate on yourself means to BE the I AM**. Psychology's solution is based on a false conclusion which is that **IT IS**. Any solution based on a False Conclusion - in this case **I AM** - can only yield poor, if any. results.

The False Self being part of the Reflection can only offer false solutions based on the false conclusion that **IT IS**.

YOUR CONCLUSIONS BIND NOBODY BUT YOU.

NISARGADATTA MAHARAJ

The conclusions and concepts that we hold bind only the "you" "you" think you are. They can never bind *you*, because **YOU ARE THAT**.

YOUR OWN CONCEPTS.
WILL ONLY SERVE AS AN INSTRUMENT
OF BONDAGE

NISARGADATTA MAHARAJ
(PG. 83, CONSCIOUSNESS AND THE ABSOLUTE)

The basic principle of Nisargadatta Maharaj, is that **"WHATEVER YOU THINK YOU ARE, YOU ARE NOT."** For this reason, as the Siva Sutras say, "Knowledge is bondage." Why? Because knowledge is, and can only be, conceptual; and, as a concept, it can only lead to more concepts and abstractions, and hence further away from the **I AM** and the **CONSCIOUSNESS** the **I AM** is made of.

In this way, all psycho-spiritual practices are done by the False Self. This "gets people" nowhere because the person's existence is only a reflection of **CONSCIOUSNESS** through the **I AM** and is based on three False Conclusions: 1) that it is; 2) that it is separate from the **I AM**; and 3) that they are made of different substances than **CONSCIOUSNESS.**

Once the reflection believes **IT IS**, soon it imagines it is separate and real, and the False Self becomes determined to look for positive outcomes and reframes. It not only re-enforces the illusion that *it is*, but keeps "one" away from the child principle wherein the formation of the root of the existence of **I AM** occurred and away from that **CONSCIOUSNESS**, which the **I AM** is made of.

Question: Why then do you teach Quantum Psychology if it is done by the False Self?

Stephen: Because as a preliminary-preparatory step it gets people into questioning everything. Unfortunately people thought this was Quantum Psychology, when it was not. This has to be understood, that *there is no False Core-False Self.* The False Core-False Self is merely a way to get people to look a what they imagine they are - so they can go beyond their whole psychology, and, ultimately, beyond **I AM**.

Question: How do you know if enquiry is being done by a False Self or it is just happening?

Stephen: If it is occurring without any intention of getting something then it is just happening. If it is being done to get something, then it is a survival produced False Self response of the nervous system.

Question: Many people feel that the False Core-False Self is true and real?

Stephen: Yes, but what I do, I tell people - particularly psychologists – that *they are not*, nor is there, a False Core. They nod their heads and want more techniques to dazzle their clients and re-enforce their own False Self in an attempt to overcome their False Core. Unfortunately, in the process, they unknowingly re-enforce their own False Solution and False Cause Conclusions.

This is one of the reasons I have stopped teaching Quantum Psychology, except to a few people. The False Self likes to have techniques and refuses to confront basic misconceptions of the **I AM**. It is difficult to get people to just look at the False Core problem rather than the techniques which they can use to resist the problem, not to mention the **I AM**.

Question: What do you do to go beyond this problem in the mind?

Stephen: Stay in the **I AM** and discard all else.

Question: So all psychology and spirituality is a reflection of **CONSCIOUSNESS** only and trying to *improve yourself* only re-enforces the imaginary self?

Stephen: Ultimately, yes.

Three

THE BODY

. . . .

WHERE THERE IS VITAL BREATH, THE
KNOWLEDGE OF I AM IS PRESENT.
THERE BEING NO VITAL BREATH, THE
KNOWLEDGE OF I AMNESS IS ABSENT.
. . . ALL WORLDLY ACTIONS ARE
GOING ON ONLY BECAUSE OF THE
KNOWLEDGE OF I AM TOGETHER
WITH THAT MOTIVE FORCE WHICH IS
THE LIFE FORCE, THE VITAL BREATH.
THIS IS NOT APART FROM YOU; YOU
ARE THAT ONLY. INVESTIGATE AND
STUDY THAT ONLY.

NISARGADATTA MAHARAJ
(Pg. 178, The Ultimate Medicine)

THE EGO (I-DENTITIES)
AND THE BODY

At one level, it can be said that the ego or our I-dentities is a by-product of the biochemistry and the nervous system of the body. The nervous system is self-re-enforcing. The nervous system omits billions of stimuli and selects-out only a fraction of stimuli and produces I-dentities or "I's", or what "you" call "you", which are a by-product of the nervous system. For this reason, I-dentities take-in very little. Everything is interpreted (digested) to keep the self and ego alive. In this way, the functioning of the ego is part of the body's survival mechanism.

It could be said that all stimuli - both internal and external are eaten and digested like food. The purpose of food, of course, is to keep the body alive. The ego, a by-product of the body, does the same thing. The ego operates on two dimension: Producing internal stimuli, i.e., fantasies, etc.; and receiving externally, i.e., interactions which it then digests to aid in its daily stimulation and survival.

For this reason, it is both very rare and very fair to say that for almost everyone, the taking-in and digesting of "enlightened" perceptions, which destroy the hold of the ego, is highly unusual.

Instead of directly taking-in and digesting pure understanding, the ego, being part of the body's nervous system, behaves like a trapped animal fighting for its life. It either seeks out input (food) even if it might poison its (the ego's) survival (I-dentity); or it runs away (flight) from it, and then develops a psychological justification for this defensive behavior. For example, if an I-dentity believes in something about itself, even if it is inaccurate, when it is confronted with an "enlightened understanding," the I-dentity as part of the nervous system cannot digest this foreign object. Instead, like the immune system, it either fights it, or the nervous system over-generalizes, *mistakenly* making it the same as "other" previously taken-in perceptions, so it does not feel threatened and it can digest it.

All perceptions that are contrary to the I-dentity are seen as a threat or attack, that must be either fought or run away from in order for the I-dentity to survive.

Furthermore, all of this is meant in *no critical way*, because "you" and all "you" call "yourself", even the **I AM**, is body-nervous system related. And as such, there is no person, just a bio-chemical, electrical reaction. In this way, a nervous system can and will, for the most part, only choose, and go for that which re-enforces itself. There is no person doing it. The concept of a person doing this or that getting blame or praise for this or that is an abstration of the nervous system and arises much later, after billions of stimuli have been omitted and only a small fraction selected-out which supports and re-enforces the "I-dentities'" survival. However, if *pure* non-dual understanding does enter into the system, like a virus, it can destroy all concepts - the sense of "I", "me", the "ego", and, ultimately, the **I AM**.

MY WORDS, IF ABSORBED,
DESTROY ALL OTHER CONCEPTS AND WORDS.

NISARGADATTA MAHARAJ

THE BODY AND THE FIVE ELEMENTS

As Nisargadatta Maharaj always said, the body was subject to, and a play of, the five elements (earth, air, water, fire and ether). Or in the language of Quantum Psychology, the body and all we call "I" are made up of a combination of the physics dimensions and forces (energy, space, mass, time, gravity, electromagnetics, etc.).

IS THERE A BODY

The body, and/or your *vision* of the body, and your perception of the world – is a must to question and understand.

To begin with, although not educated in neuro-science, Nisargadatta Maharaj was intuitively and *apperceptually* aware of the field, and especially of the work of Alfred Korzybski, the founder of General Semantics. Korzybski (1933) demonstrated in his *structural differential* that the Quantum level or **VOID** cannot be perceived by the body, i.e., the nervous system. So too the microscopic level cannot be perceived by the body's nervous system. The world of objects however can only be perceived by the nervous system.

In order for the body's nervous system to perceive a simple object, like the book you are reading, requires that the body *omit* billions of stimuli, and *select-out* only a small fraction in order for this "you" to perceive this book as solid.

But is the book actually real and solid? *No.* Because the perceiv*er* of the book is part of the nervous system and hence part of it's abstracting (omitting and selecting out) process. This omitting and selecting out process of the nervous system makes the book appear solid to a nervous system's perceiv*er* of it. In other words, the perceiv*er* of the body is part of the nervous system, and hence the perceiv*er* perceives and then experiences a solid body and book where there is none.

Now what does this say about the perceiv*er*'s perception of your hand and arm holding this book?

The hand and arm too are perceived by the nervous system's perceiv*er*. This means that the arm and hand are a result of, and appear because of, a perceiv*er*. The perceiv*er* too, as an abstraction of the nervous system, is non-existent. In other words, all is a result of the abstracting (omitting and selecting out process) of the nervous system. If there were no nervous system, then there would be no perceiv*er* or perception of the body, and hence no I-dentity or view of the world.

This has been summarized by the sanskrit *DRISTI SHRISTI VADA*, which says that the world is only there as long as there is a perceiv*er* (you) there to perceive it. Why? Because the perceiv*er* "you" is a by-product of the nervous system.

This could lead us into a rather shocking realization. That the conclusions, which a perceiv*er* has about the body - like it is solid or exists in a specific location—are perceiv*er*-perceiv*ed*-based understandings only—all of which is a conclusion and a further abstraction of the nervous system and it's perceiv*er*, which means it is further away from the Quantum level. Since all perception can only occur if there is a perceiv*er* there, and since the perceiv*er* and its perception (even of the body) are by-products of the omitting and selecting out process of the nervous system, then, if there is no-perceiv*er*, then there is no-you. *In this way, we could say that liberation is not liberation from the body, but the realization that there is no body.*

PRIOR TO THE PERCEIVER
WAS CONSCIOUSNESS

Prior to the perceiver or as Nisargadatta Maharaj put it,

"8 DAYS BEFORE CONCEPTION—
WHO WERE YOU?"

This state of no perception or *un*awareness requires *ap-perception* prior to the perceiver of the body and body consciousness.

The "I am not the body," the pillar of yoga, can best be seen in this context. In short, **CONSCIOUSNESS** is *prior* to the body. This **CONSCIOUSNESS** has identified with the perceiver-body rather than itself as **CONSCIOUSNESS**, which is **UNDIFFERENTIATED** and prior to the perceiver.

UNLESS THE CONSCIOUSNESS IS THERE, THE BODY IS NOT. IN DEEP SLEEP WE ARE NOT AWARE OF THE BODY, WE ARE AWARE OF THE BODY ONLY WHEN WE AWAKE AND THE CONSCIOUSNESS IS THERE. THERE-FORE WHEN I SAY THIS, I MEAN THAT IT IS THIS CONSCIOUSNESS WHICH I AM, NOT THE BODY WHICH COMES LATER.

NISARGADATTA MAHARAJ

(Pg. 37, Consciousness and the Absolute)

In this way, "I" recently *apperceived* that "I" was not. Upon awakening "I" was. This is why Ramana Maharishi pointed to the state between deep sleep and waking as moving from **I AM NOT** to **I AM**. It is the "space" where the **CONSCIOUSNESS** is not body identified so we sleep. When the **CONSCIOUSNESS** is body identified, or **I AM** identified, we are awake.

Furthermore, the perception by a percei*ver* that there is a body and an "I", by the percei*ver* of the body, is also concocted (abstracted and assumed) by a percei*ver*, which also is an abstraction of the nervous system, or a percei*ver*'s viewing it's perceived (the body in this case). The nervous system's further abstracting creates the illusion of solidness and **I AM**, and this (the body) is "me".

The *mirage*, or the solidified image, is a construction of the Nervous System's abstracting process. The Nervous System, which is a condensation of **CONSCIOUSNESS**, creates through the abstracting process the illusion of solidness where there is none. This is the *mirage* or the illusion of an object and the body where there is none.

THE BODY-MIND COMPLEX IS MOSTLY AN OBJECT, A PHENOMENON, AND NO PHENOMENON CAN ACT. . . . YOU WILL NEVER BE ABLE GRASP YOUR TRUE NATURE, FOR THIS, THE CENTER OF PERCEPTION MUST CHANGE. IF THE CENTER OF PERCEPTION IS A PHENOMENON, THEN WHATEVER WAY YOU LOOK, THAT LOOKING IS STILL FROM THE CENTER OF PHENOMENON. SO UNLESS THE CENTER OF PERCEIVING ITSELF IS CHANGED TO THE NOUMENON, YOU WILL NEVER GET . . . YOUR TRUE NATURE.

NISARGADATTA MAHARAJ
(Pg. 97-98, The Ultimate Medicine)

NO PERCEIVER NO WORLD

In this way the perceiv*er* of your world and the world you perceive are created by the nervous system.

The perceiv*er* of this world and the body are one and the same. Any assumptions or abstractions by the perceiv*er* occurs *after the fact* and *after the experience has already taken place* and are further abstracted and only serve to enable the body's survival to re-enforce its false understanding.

Simply put, the perceiv*er* is part of the nervous system and an abstraction of the nervous system. Its perception of the body and the world exist only as long as this phantom phenomena of perceiv*er* and perceiv*ed* are there. Its view of the world is far from the Quantum level and hence, since it omits billions of stimuli and selects out just a small fraction, the perceiv*er* perceives a solid world where there is no solid world. Furthermore, when the perceiv*er* draws conclusions about its world, it (the perceiv*er*) further abstracts from its original perception, thus moving it further and further and further away from the Quantum Level and the **VOID of UNDIFFERENTIATED CONSCIOUSNESS.**

WHATEVER THE EXPERIENCER FEELS OR THINKS IS ALL IN CONSCIOUSNESS AND IS NOT REAL.

NISARGADATTA MAHARAJ
(Consciousness and the Absolute)

THE BODY AND
THE VITAL BREATHE

IN ORDER TO REALLY UNDERSTAND YOU HAVE TO WORSHIP THAT PRANA, THE VITAL FORCE.

NISARGADATTA MAHARAJ

Where do we go from here? Within the body we know and experience the breath. Certainly meditation, which focuses on breathing and on the space between two breathes, is commonly practiced throughout the Eastern and now Western world. However, contained within this breath is *prana*, and within that *prana* lies the *vital force* we call life. It is through focusing on that life force and on our vital breath, that the **I AM** is *apperceived*. It is this life force which *animates* the breathing apparatus, and gives the life illusion to the mirage-body.

When one stays with the life force or vital breath, discarding all else, the **I AM**, inner-self, or God, is *realized*.

IT IS THIS LIFE FORCE'S CONSCIOUS PRESENCE WITHOUT FORM WHICH HAS BEEN CALLED GOD.

NISARGADATTA MAHARAJ
(Pg. 166, Ultimate Medicine)

It is through this focus on the Life Force or vital breath - *not the breathing* which it is commonly misunderstood to be, but rather the vital force or that which is "behind" or "underneath" the breathing, and which animates the breathing – that the **I AM** is realized. More importantly, through this deep humility, a relief and a laugh develops because, as the ego vanishes, we realize something quite simple, beautiful, and opposite to many teachings we have received from outside of ourselves.

YOU ARE NOTHING BETTER THAN VEGETATION, LIKE GRASS GROWING, HUMAN BEINGS ARE GROWING.

NISARGADATTA MAHARAJ
(Pg. 45, Consciousness of the Absolute)

Four

THE KNOWER
AND THE WITNESS

· ·

IF IN THE STATE OF WITNESSING
YOU ASK YOURSELF: "WHO AM I?"
THE ANSWER COMES AT ONCE;
THOUGH IT IS WORDLESS AND SILENT.

NISARGADATTA MAHARAJ
(Pg. 303, I Am That)

THE WITNESS

Probably for reasons of language two words which often get confused are the WITNESS and the observer. The observer observes and the observer is also an experiencer and a knower of what is occurring. At first it appears as though there is one knower-observer. However, upon investigation, we discover an infinite number of observers or knowers, each arising and subsiding with each new thought or experience. This understanding explains Nisargadatta Maharaj's saying;

"ANYTHING YOU KNOW ABOUT YOU CANNOT BE."

NISARGADATTA MAHARAJ

Why? Because if a thought of "I hate myself" arises, a new "knower" ("I", "observer") arises with that thought. This means that the observer or knower and the thought arise and subside together as one solid unit. Although they appear as separate, they are as inseparable as the rays of the sun from the sun. In this way, if I know about a thought - I am the knower of a thought; and since; I am not the known thought, neither am I the knower of the thought.

Once one enquires into the nature of the knower, or as the Bhagavad Gita says; "To know the knower", the knower-known, or observer-observed, disappears. Furthermore, the knower, and all the knowledge the knower knows, also disappears. It is upon the disappearance of the knower-known or observer-observed dyad that the **WITNESS** is realized.

To Illustrate - or as Maharaj called it, "appreceive"—let's, explore this Enquiry below:

ENQUIRY

Enquiry Step I   Notice a thought.

Enquiry Step II   Be the knower of the thought.

Enquiry Step III   Notice what occurs when "I" ask,
                       "What knower is knowing that?"

Most people go into the blank non-verbal **I AM**, or as I have said to students, "Notice a difference between you and the knower". They usually go beyond into the pure blankness of **I AM** and/or the **WITNESS**, beyond the knower-known dyad.

Nisargadatta Maharaj once said to me; "Who is the knower of the knowledge of your birth?" At first, I could not answer. A few hours later, I realized I am the knower of the knowledge of my birth. Years later, the knower, the **I AM**, and even the **WITNESS** of that knower, evaporated into **NOTHINGNESS**. Why? Because each knower only has a limited or separate knowing or knowledge which is unique and limited to only that specific knower.

Once you are beyond the knower-known dyad the knower and known, along with the knower's knowledge disappears, and "you", the **WITNESS**, are beyond them.

THE KNOWER

The knower-experiencer-observer and the act of know-ing-experiencing-observing and what the knower knows the experiencer experiences and the observer observes - are all one solid unit. This includes the Thinker, the Feeler, the Sensator, and the Perceiver along with what is thought, felt, sensed, or perceived, and the act of thinking feeling, sensing and perceiving.

They are one solid, inseparable, holographic unit, mean-ing one is contained within the other. From a physics perspective, Heisenberg demonstrated that you cannot separate the observer from the observed. For the sake of this dialogue, therefore, I will use the term knower or perceiver to denote all of the above.

With an infinite number of knowers-perceivers, i.e., each perception contains a new and different perceiver, etc., there is an infinite number of possible knowns and perceptions.

In this way, all that is perceived, even the perceiver of the *mirage*, is a phenomena and part of the *mirage* itself. "Perception" and knowledge occur to a specific knower-perceiver within the *mirage* and thus remain in that knower's-knowledge. In this way, you can say that you are not it (the knower-known) but rather you are **THAT**, which *appears* to be this (the knower-known). This appearance of a separate knower-perceiver, etc., is an illusion and is contained within the *mirage* only.

Therefore, all knowers-perceivers-known-perceived need to be *apperceived* as **NOT-THIS**. This is the Vedanta of it. This "giving-up" of knower-experiencer-known-experiences does not occur often. Although there appears to be an "I" who gives them up or takes them on, this "I" is only part of these phenomenological structures which **IS NOT**.

SORTING OUT AND DISCARDING ARE ABSOLUTELY NECESSARY. EVERYTHING MUST BE SCRUTINIZED AND THE UNNECESSARY RUTHLESSLY DESTROYED. BELIEVE ME, THERE CANNOT BE TOO MUCH DESTRUCTION.

NISARGADATTA MAHARAJ

(Pg. 84, I Am That)

It must be understood that **THAT EATS** (or thins-out) "I" **CONSCIOUSNESS**, and that this includes not only awareness, but awareness of the **VOID**, and even awareness of **THAT ONE SUBSTANCE**.

THE BODY IS FOOD.

NISARGADATTA MAHARAJ

In the process of eating and digesting (dissolving), there is a loss of "I" consciousness. However, ultimately, this goes unnoticed because the noticer-noticing-noticed are no longer present.

THE WITNESS

WHEN THE KNOWER IS SEEN AS SEPARATE FROM THE KNOWN, THE WITNESS STANDS ALONE; WHEN THE KNOWN AND KNOWER ARE SEEN AS ONE, THE WITNESS BECOMES ONE WITH THEM.

NISARGADATTA MAHARAJ

This rather complex statement describes the subtle difference between the **WITNESS** and the observer. If the observer or knower is seen as separate from the observed-known, then there is really no **WITNESSING**. However, when the observer-observed or knower-known are seen as one then there is just a **WITNESSING**.

ENQUIRY

Enquiry Step I   Be the observer of a thought.

Enquiry Step II   *Apperceive* that the observer and thought are made of the same substance.

When the observer and observed or knower-known are apperceived or apprehended as the same substance, we go beyond the observer-observed, knower-known dyad into the **WITNESS**, which is beyond the observer-observed, knower-known, and the illusion that they are separate and different substances.

THE WITNESS IS A BRIDGE BETWEEN THE SUPREME AND THE MANIFOLD CONSCIOUSNESS OF A PERSON.

NISARGADATTA MAHARAJ

One of the primary questions is always, "Why so much emphasis on the **I AM**?" Nisargadatta Maharaj stressed this because the **I AM** and its **WITNESSING PRESENCE**, when "stayed with" or turned around, propels one to "fall back," expanding out until the **BIG EMPTINESS** and the **NOT-I-I** is realized.

BEYOND THE WITNESS THERE IS AN INFINITE EMPTINESS.

NISARGADATTA MAHARAJ

(PG,. 355, I AM THAT)

AN ENQUIRY INTO AWARENESS

Question: Can you state the difference between awareness and consciousness?

Stephen: Everything in the *mirage* is made of **CONSCIOUS-NESS**. Awareness is that which is aware of this interaction of what has been called, the *play of consciousness*. Pure Awareness has no subject-object and no awar*er* or awar*ee* involved. It does not care, intrude, or, in short, is not bothered with, or by, **CONSCIOUSNESS**.

Question: Why does awareness not care or want to change **CONSCIOUSNESS**?

Stephen: Because, as Baba Prakashananda used to say, "Shakti (consciousness) is maya (illusion). In pure awareness, there is no subject-object.

Question: There are some schools who try to enhance awareness?

Stephen: These schools confuse awareness with observation. Observation, which is part of **CONSCIOUSNESS** and hence contains the virus of wanting to change, along with judgment, evaluation, significance, preferences, and the illusion of volition. Awareness is beyond observation or the observer-observed relationship.

Question: Would it be fair to say that a goal is to not have judgment?

Stephen: *No*. To have or not have judgment is a function of the observer-observed dyad. Awareness is beyond observer and observed.

Question: So judgments do not disappear?

Stephen: Judgments are a function of the observer and observed, on one level, and the nervous system on another. And though they may still continue, this has nothing to do with anything. If you try to reform the judgemental person, you are buying into or believing there is a person and a body.

Question: But teachers seem to judge all sorts of things.

Stephen: Yes, and the mind-body machinery of the observer-observed dyad continues even though a "teacher" is **BEYOND CONSCIOUSNESS**. You could say it is part of the body-mind.

ENQUIRY

This demonstration is an attempt to look at, and dismantle the concepts associated with awareness.

Wolinsky: Where in the body do you experience the **I AM** concept?

Student: My eyes.

Wolinsky: How does the **I AM** concept define awareness?

Student: Awareness observes.

Wolinsky: *If* that was just a concept that the **I AM** had about awareness and had nothing to do with anything _____?

Student: I go blank.

Wolinsky: What other concepts does the **I AM** concept have about the concept of awareness?

Student: That awareness can change things.

Wolinsky: *If* that was just a concept that the concept of **I AM** had about awareness and had nothing to do with anything then _____?

Student: Blank_____.

Wolinsky: What other concept does the concept of **I AM** have about the concept of awareness?

Student: That it is awareness?

Wolinsky: *If* that was just a concept that the concept of **I AM** had about the concept of awareness and it had nothing to do with anything, what is the *apperception*?

Student: _____Blank.

Note:
Notice that we use the term, *concept of I AM,* and concept of awareness in an attempt to go beyond the **I AM**.

Wolinsky: What lies has the concept of awareness told itself?

Student: That it is.

Wolinsky: Why would the concept of awareness come up with
             the concept of *IS*?

Student: Silence, _____. Blank.

Wolinsky: If awareness were just a concept and a lens and you
             were not it, what is *apperceived*?

Student: Absolutely blank_____Silence.

Wolinsky: What lie could the concept of awareness tell the con-
             cept of **EMPTINESS**?

Student;   That it is.

Wolinsky: Why would the concept of awareness come up with
             the lie or concept of **IS**?

Student: There is neither awareness nor **EMPTINESS**.

Wolinsky: Why would the concept of awareness come up with
             that lie?

Student: _____Long silence.

Note:

Any enquiry presupposes that it is: like awareness,
emptiness, etc., which is not true. When a student
asked Nisargadatta who am I? he replied:

"EIGHT DAYS BEFORE CONCEPTION, WHO WERE YOU?" ... UNAWARENESS.

NISARGADATTA MAHARAJ

Five

THE REALIZATION

. . . .

THERE IS NOT SUCH THING AS
ENLIGHTENMENT. THE APPRECIATION
OF THIS FACT IS ITSELF
ENLIGHTENMENT.

NISARGADATTA MAHARAJ

THE ENLIGHTENMENT FANTASY

Enlightenment, like most other concepts, is misunderstood by many people. Enlightenment has come to be *described* as everything from eternal bliss to omniscience from blue light to being a guru, and from pure wisdom to unconditional love. The list goes on and on and on.

Let us begin by clearly stating: First, for someone to say *"I" am enlightened* would require a separate "I" to declare it is so.

REALIZATION IS OF THE FACT
THAT YOU ARE NOT A PERSON

NISARGADATTA MAHARAJ

(Pg., 441 I Am That)

Second, the person is a concept, a phenomena, a reflection of **CONSCIOUSNESS**, and, as such, is merely an image made of **CONSCIOUSNESS**, which ultimately *is not*. So how can a person be enlightened.

Third, many people imagine the concept of enlightenment as a magic bullet which takes away all pain forever. Furthermore, enlightenment and bondage are concepts which exist *only* within the *mirage*. In other words; *you are a mirage who does not know you are a mirage*. Therefore, *anything* experienced or known about is part of that *mirage* including you and all "you" call "yourself".

THERE CAN BE
NO PERSON WHO IS SELF-REALIZED

NISARGADATTA MAHARAJ

If we were to imply a non-existent person can realize something, it would be like imagining a reflection in a mirror could realize enlightenment. The concept of a person who has realized something is only from the point of view of a *mirage-self* looking; and, hence, seeing or viewing another *mirage-self* as realized, neither of the two exists.

In this way, it would be like a *mirage* in the desert thinking or imagining it is alive, with life, choices, a past, that it is in bondage, and that some way, if it does the right thing, it will become enlightened. The concept of enlightenment exists only to the *mirage* person.

Nisargadatta, without concern for a person's ideas, confronted these concepts and brought them to the surface so that the *mirage* of water (person) could begin to evaporate.

This evaporation of droplets of water (or concepts) occurs through investigation of all we hold dear – including God, Guru and Enlightenment.

The most we could say is that enlightenment is the realization that everything is made of **THAT SAME SUBSTANCE**. Call it **VOID, NOTHINGNESS, CONSCIOUSNESS**, or whatever.

However, there is no *separate individual* enlightenment to the enlightened, because to the enlightened, the water droplets of concepts and the **I AM** have evaporated. They no longer are a *mirage* not knowing they are a *mirage*; they are **NOTHING** or **THAT**, *but not as a "thing" or an "it" or an "I"*.

PERSONAL ENTITY AND
ENLIGHTENMENT CANNOT GO TOGETHER

NISARGADATTA MAHARAJ

The concept of a personal individual self is a concept which is non-existent. The illusion that an individual self gets enlightened is like imagining that a picture on a piece of paper can become an Olympic swimmer.

Enlightenment, which contains the illusion of a magic bullet that takes away all pain, is one of the greatest illusions of the *mirage*. Bondage, liberation, enlightenment. and an individual "you" which somehow possesses it, are all contained within the *mirage*

Nisargadatta Maharaj said, "**YOU ARE THE CHILD OF A BARREN WOMEN.**" In the same way to believe in individual enlightenment is to believe in the child of a barren woman attaining something. Once this enlightenment concept evaporates as part of the *mirage*, there is no more striving for *IT*. The illusion of an *IT* and a **YOU** getting *IT* are gone. Moreover, the illusion that I will find out who I am disappears because there is **NO I THAT YOU ARE**.

ENQUIRY

Wolinsky: Where is the **I AM** concept located?

Student: My eyes.

Wolinsky: Ask the **I AM** concept to define a person.

Student: An individual human being.

Wolinsky: And what assumptions has the **I AM** concept made about that?

Student: That it is, and where I am.

Wolinsky: And if the concept of **IS** and "where" were just concepts of **I AM** and had nothing to do with anything?

Student: _____Blank

Wolinsky: This **CONSCIOUSNESS**, which "views" through the concept of **I AM** which believes this, how has it deceived itself?

Student: Believing itself that it was separate.

Wolinsky: And if the concept of separate were concepts of the
                CONSCIOUSNESS "viewing" through the **I AM**
                was untrue _____?

Student: _____Blank.

Wolinsky: Regarding **CONSCIOUSNESS** having this concept
                of a person, any unacknowledged communication?

Student: That **IT IS**.

Wolinsky: And if that concept called **IT IS** had nothing to do
                with anything _____?

Student: _____Blank.

Wolinsky: Anything this **CONSCIOUSNESS** "viewing"
                through the concept of **I AM** must not know?

Student: That it is a concept.

Wolinsky: Anything it must not experience?

Student: _____It isn't.

Wolinsky: Now?

Student: _____Blank. Gone.
                _____Silence

THAT HAPPENS OR IT DOESN'T

THAT *just happens*, it is not personal like an achievement
or something to be gotten or a prize to be proud of. Once
Nisargadatta said,

IN INDIA THERE WERE FLOODS UP NORTH NEAR DELHI—CAN YOU TAKE PRIDE IN THAT?

The same is true of enlightenment, it is not personally up to a "you". The form becomes **EMPTINESS, EMPTINESS** becomes form. In that process, polarities as Patanjali called them, occur. However, it is still form becoming **EMPTINESS, EMPTINESS** becoming form.

Question: It seems that enlightenment just doesn't happen to anyone. It seems to be a process, and to occur within someone who has done some form of spiritual practice.

Stephen: Theoretically, it can happen anywhere to anyone. But, for the most part, it seems to take root and to stabilize within one who has done a practice for some time. There are exceptions; there can be no rules. Ramana Maharishi is a freak example of this.

REALIZATION ON THE SPOT IS RARE, IT USUALLY REQUIRES SOME FORM OF RIPENING

NISARGADATTA MAHARAJ

Question: So it could happen to anyone?

Stephen: Theoretically, yes, however if it happened to you suddenly, you would probably go crazy. It would be difficult for the body-mind and nervous system to handle it. Notice when Ramana Maharishi realized, he suddenly left home and sat for years and years in meditation. He was found and named Ramana Maharishi - he sat with it for years. It did not happen and suddenly he was selling himself as enlightened,

asking for money, giving workshops, and handing
out certificates. This is why Nisargadatta Maharaj
described the process this way;

LIKE A FRUIT IT TAKES A LONG TIME TO RIPEN, BUT IT DROPS SUDDENLY

NISARGADATTA MAHARAJ

Question: Is this why you use Quantum Psychology as a path?

Stephen: Quantum Psychology is not a path it is preparation
only. There are no paths to **THAT**. You cannot throw
seeds at rocks and expect them to grow into plants.
In the same way, Quantum Psychology clears the
rocks and weeds so that plants can grow.

Question: Then it is a path?

Stephen: No, all paths which guarantee results are misleading
at best and are bullshit at worst. *Nobody can guarantee results.* All paths are born of knowledge - therefore there must be a know*er*. People imagine there
is a path when there is none. You are beyond the
know*er* and the knowledge that the know*er* has.

Question: So Quantum Psychology or mantra is preparation?

Stephen: As a *general* rule, it is a place to start - soon it might
fall away - but whether this thing called enlighten-
ment comes or not - it is not *caused* by something a
"you" might do. It happens like lightning – it might
strike or it might not.

Question: But I do dismantle identities in hopes of going beyond?

Stephen: At first, the "I" or enquir*er* imagines it does this or
                that. Soon "you" *apperceive* that the **VOID** is do-
                ing, that no "I" does anything. The "I" is merely thin-
                ning out "I"-dentities. You do nothing. Eventually
                *you apperceive that there is no VOID doing and there
                is NO-Doer.*

Question: Then you go beyond?

Stephen: There is no beyond as in a location - it is merely a
                word, and, unfortunately, words create images. There
                is no location, no space, no permanent bliss, and **NO-
                I** to say, "This is it." This is why *Not-this-Not-this,*
                or as Nisargadatta Maharaj said, "*It is not perceiv-
                able or conceivable,*" that there is no know*er*-knowl-
                edge or knowing there - and there is no there, it is
                beyond and is NOT, because in order to be there,
                there would have to be a be-*er* there to say, "This is
                it." Since there is No-be-er there, **THERE IS NO
                IT**. *The great illusion is that you will find out who
                you are. But there is no-I that you find out you are—*
                it all disappears upon investigation. *This is the great
                illusion, that you will find out who you are— but
                you won't because you are NOT.*

IT IS PRIOR TO THE KNOWLEDGE OF I AM,
BUT THERE IS NO PRIOR;
YOU CAN NEVER SAY WHAT IT IS,
ONLY WHAT IT ISN'T.

NISARGADATTA MAHARAJ

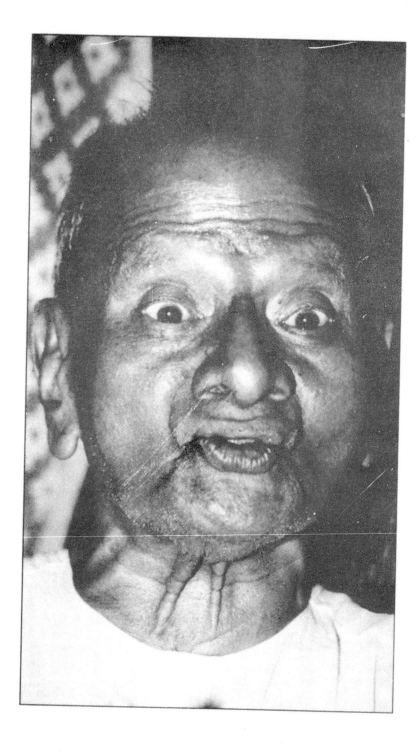

Six

CONSCIOUSNESS

· ·

WHEN YOU KNOW THE SOURCE OF THIS
BEINGNESS OR "I" CONSCIOUSNESS THAT
IS LIBERATION

NISARGADATTA MAHARAJ

(Pg. 42, The Ultimate Medicine)

The source of **"I"** is **I AM**, but the source of **I AM** is **CONSCIOUSNESS.**

CONSCIOUSNESS →*I AM.* **CONSCIOUSNESS** "becomes" and is the **I AM.**

What is **CONSCIOUSNESS?**. The 10th century poet and saint, Janeshwar Maharaj, called **CONSCIOUSNESS** the divine substance.

CONSIDER THIS BEINGNESS OR CONSCIOUSNESS AS THE SUPREME GOD.

NISARGADATTA MAHARAJ
(PG. 68, THE ULTIMATE MEDICINE)

Nisargadatta Maharaj says that we should abide in **I AM,** and that this "leads" to **CONSCIOUSNESS** which is the source of **I AM.** He said to worship **CONSCIOUSNESS** as God. Why? Because even the concept of God is contained within the *mirage* and is part of the play of that divine substance or **CONSCIOUSNESS.** The **CONSCIOUSNESS** which the Non-verbal **I AM** is made of is **GOD,** and is the source of the "outer" or "inner" **GOD.** To understand what he meant, we need to look at it from several vantage points.

CONSCIOUSNESS: THE SUBSTANCE OF THE MIRAGE

CONSCIOUSNESS is the substance that the *mirage* is made of. In this way, all you see, feel, think, all "others," and all paths - even the concept of God – are all concepts made of **CONSCIOUSNESS.**

It is this **CONSCIOUSNESS,** which if it were not there, then there would be no **I AM** or a **GOD.** Better said, when **CON-**

SCIOUSNESS realizes there is only **CONSCIOUSNESS**, then there is no **I AM** or God. Why? Because with only one substance, there is no **CONSCIOUSNESS** to *realize* there is only **CON-SCIOUSNESS.**

The question is; How do we discover **WHO WE ARE.** Nisargadatta Maharaj continually said that when someone came to see him, they should understand that there is not an "I" who is asking a question, and a "him" (Nisargadatta Maharaj) who is answering the question. There is only **CONSCIOUSNESS** "speaking."

THE CONSCIOUSNESS OF ENQUIRY

Enquiry occurs when **CONSCIOUSNESS** "changes its direction" from being extroverted, and looking to the outside and identifying with its reflections as *"I"*, to dis-identifying with *"I"* and identifying with **CONSCIOUSNESS.** When this occurs, **CON-SCIOUSNESS,** turns upon itself. This introversion of **CON-SCIOUSNESS** forces I-dentities to disappear, as a *mirage* in the desert disappears upon investigation. In this way, Enquiry, which leads from the I-dentification with reflections to **I AM,** and then from **I AM** to **CONSCIOUSNESS,** is the worship of **CON-SCIOUSNESS**

THE WORSHIPER IS IN THE CONSCIOUSNESS, AND THE OBJECT OF WORSHIP IS ALSO CONSCIOUSNESS.

NISARGADATTA MAHARAJ

(Pg. 71, Consciousness And The Absolute)

THE PLAY OF CONSCIOUSNESS

CONSCIOUSNESS is the substance that the *mirage* is made of. To call it the play of CONSCIOUSNESS clearly says it all. But, what does that mean? That can best be summed up by the statement of Baba Prakashanada, that "shakti (CONSCIOUS-NESS) is maya. This statement reveals a simple but profound truth: CONSCIOUSNESS is both the substance of the *mirage*; and, as the substance of the *mirage*, CONSCIOUSNESS itself plays the part of a "you" and a "me". It plays the part of I AM, and it is the substance that the I AM is made of. You could say that the I AM is a by-product of CONSCIOUSNESS and that CONSCIOUSNESS is *prior* to I AM.

The question is often asked, "Shouldn't we worship CON-SCIOUSNESS as many suggest?" Absolutely, but what is worship? Worship occurs when we focus our entire attention on the source of the I AM *apperceiving* that any "I" thought, or any experience are themselves made of CONSCIOUSNESS. When this occurs, the very concept disappears and there is just CONSCIOUS-NESS. When CONSCIOUSNESS is worshipped (focused upon) with undying attention, "we" are catapulted beyond CONSCIOUS-NESS itself to no CONSCIOUSNESS or NOTHINGNESS.

I WANT YOU TO DWELL ON THE BORDERLINE OF CONSCIOUSNESS AND NO-CONSCIOUSNESS

NISARGADATTA MAHARAJ
(Pg. 57, Consciousness And The Absolute)

Prior to CONSCIOUSNESS is this "place." It is "before the arising of the illusion of CONSCIOUSNESS or the *mirage*. This is why Nisargadatta Maharaj stressed *prior* to CONSCIOUS-NESS

THE TOTAL ABSENCE OF ALL KNOWLEDGE OR IGNORANCE IS THAT STATE PRIOR TO THE ARISING OF CONSCIOUSNESS.

NISARGADATTA MAHARAJ

(Pg. 88, Consciousness And The Absolute)

In this way, the glue that holds the *mirage* together is **I AM**. But the substance that the **I AM** is made of is **CONSCIOUSNESS**. This is why Nisargadatta Maharaj repeats again and again to focus on the **I AM** as a gateway or portal to this "understanding", *apperception* or *realization*.

CONSCIOUSNESS

TO RECAPITULATE: FIRST, I AM NOT EVEN CONSCIOUS. I DO NOT KNOW THAT I EXIST. THEN, THIS CONSCIOUSNESS FORCES ITSELF ON THAT STATE OF UNAWARENESS TO AN EXTENT THAT WE BEGIN TO FEEL THAT WE ARE CONSCIOUS. FINALLY, IT FORCES ITSELF INTO FULL CONSCIOUSNESS, AND I KNOW THAT I EXIST, I AM THERE. AND THAT BECOMES A CONCEPT, FROM WHICH STARTS THE ENTIRE WORLD OF TROUBLES. IN THAT ORIGINAL STATE WHEN YOU ARE NOT AWARE, THERE IS NO TROUBLE OF ANY KIND. BUT ONCE THIS CONSCIOUSNESS MAKES ITS PRESENCE

FELT, ALL THE TROUBLE STARTS. THIS
IS NOT MINE, I KNOW THIS IS NOT
MINE, BUT IT IS FORCED UPON ME,
AND THEN ALSO I BEGIN TO SAY
THAT IT IS "ME" –THIS IS THE WAY
THAT IDENTIFICATION TAKES PLACE.

NISARGADATTA MAHARAJ
(Pg. 52, The Ultimate Medicine)

It is **CONSCIOUSNESS** which *conceals* itself and **CON-SCIOUSNESS** which *reveals* itself and the nature of the *mirage*. Even the concept of time and space are made of **CONSCIOUS-NESS**, the substance or illusion of the *mirage*.

THE IDEA OF BEGINNING AND TIME ARE IN CONSCIOUSNESS.

NISARGADATTA MAHARAJ

THE BODY IS CONSCIOUSNESS

THE ONE WHO IDENTIFIES WITH THE BODY IS CONSCIOUSNESS ITSELF.

NISARGADATTA MAHARAJ
(Pg. 42, Consciousness And The Absolute)

CONSCIOUSNESS identifies itself as the body and ultimately it is a "solidified" form of CONSCIOUSNESS, but does the body exist? Only as CONSCIOUSNESS. It is CONSCIOUSNESS, which creates the illusion of solidified CONSCIOUSNESS. It is the solidified CONSCIOUSNESS, which is the body's nervous system which creates a perceiver and a perceived. It is through the eyes of this perceptual mechanism, which is part of the body and which is made of CONSCIOUSNESS, that the solidified CONSCIOUSNESS called the body and the world seem like "other" "separate" and made of different substances.

EARLIER, THE QUESTION AROSE, WHEN I SAID "CONSCIOUSNESS," DID I MEAN THE BODY? I SAID, NO, NOT THE BODY. FOR THE CONSCIOUSNESS TO APPEAR, IT NEEDS A BODY, IT NEEDS A VEHICLE, AND THE BODY IS THE FOOD FOR THIS CONSCIOUSNESS. WITHOUT FOOD, THE BODY CANNOT EXIST, AND CONSCIOUSNESS CANNOT EXIST WITHOUT THE BODY. SO THIS BODY IS THE FOOD FOR CONSCIOUSNESS TO EXIST. IF THE BODY DISAPPEARS, THE FOOD DISAPPEARS, AND THEN THE CONSCIOUSNESS WILL ALSO DISAPPEAR. THEN ALSO IT MAY BE ASKED: IS THERE ANY DIFFERENCE BETWEEN WHAT IS TERMED AS MAN OR THE SELF AND THIS CONSCIOUSNESS? IT IS THE SAME THING, BUT DIFFERENT

WORDS ARE USED IN DIFFERENT
CONTEXTS; THE CONTENT IS BASI-
CALLY THE SAME. I USE THE WORD
"TASTE," THE ESSENCE OF THE BODY;
THE TASTE OF THAT ESSENCE IS THIS
BEINGNESS, OF BEING ALIVE, AND
WANTING TO BE ALIVE. ONE LOVES
THE STATE OF BEING ALIVE AND
WANTS TO PERPETUATE IT AS LONG
AS POSSIBLE. SO THE LOVE FOR THIS
CONSCIOUSNESS IS THIS TASTE.

NISARGADATTA MAHARAJ

(Pg. 52-53, The Ultimate Medicine)

The body is there only as long as the perceiver of the body
is there. The perceiver of the body and the body are made of **CON-
SCIOUSNESS**. For this reason as long as there is a perceiver which
"sees" itself separate from the perceived, there is the illusion of
body and world. Moreover, even the *love of existence or survival*
is this **CONSCIOUSNESS**, and without the body there is no **I
AM**; and hence only **CONSCIOUSNESS**, which without a body
is not

ENQUIRY INTO THE NATURE
OF CONSCIOUSNESS

Question: How can I realize beyond body consciousness?

Stephen: When **CONSCIOUSNESS** is body identified we
                call it the waking state. When the **CONSCIOUS-
                NESS** is less body identified, we call it the dream
                state, and when the body goes into deep sleep the

CONSCIOUSNESS is no longer body identified. For example, when you lie down to sleep or take a nap. Many people say, as they begin to "leave their body," the body jerks and then they fall asleep.

What is happening is that the CONSCIOUSNESS which is body identified is losing its body identification. When this occurs, CONSCIOUSNESS, by losing its body identification, is just CONSCIOUS-NESS or "thinned out" CONSCIOUSNESS again.

When CONSCIOUSNESS stops its identification with the body, the body falls asleep. If "you", as CONSCIOUSNESS, can stay with CONSCIOUSNESS, as this occurs you *apperceive* of the state between waking and deep sleep, which is *prior* to differentiated CONSCIOUSNESS, and prior to I AM.

Question: But I cannot do that.

Stephen: Then, stay with I AM until it falls away and its source CONSCIOUSNESS will become revealed.

AWARENESS-OBSERVATION AND CONSCIOUSNESS

WHEN YOU ARE IN THE POSITION TO OBSERVE CONSCIOUSNESS, YOU ARE OUT OF CONSCIOUSNESS, THEN, YOU ARE IN WHAT WE CALL "THE AWARENESS STATE".

NISARGADATTA MAHARAJ
(PG. 156, THE ULTIMATE MEDICINE)

Awareness is prior to **CONSCIOUSNESS**. There can be awareness without **CONSCIOUSNESS**, but there can never be **CONSCIOUSNESS** without awareness.

THERE ARE LEVELS IN CONSCIOUSNESS, NOT IN AWARENESS.

NISARGADATTA MAHARAJ
(Pg. 403, I Am That)

Question: Then what is awareness of **EMPTINESS**?

Stephen: **EMPTINESS** is still **UNDIFFERENTIATED CONSCIOUSNESS**. You can call it "dead" spots or still spots within the play of **CONSCIOUSNESS**, like the eye of the hurricane, but it is still **CONSCIOUSNESS**.

Question: Nisargadatta Maharaj says I am **NOTHINGNESS**.

Stephen: Yes, he is in the eye of the hurricane. The eye being **NOTHINGNESS**, the hurricane being **CONSCIOUSNESS**. But still, the eye of the hurricane is part of, and made of the same substance as, the hurricane. And it is from this eye that **CONSCIOUSNESS** can be *apperceived* more clearly. Once Nisargadatta Maharaj said to me, *"Does Muktananda discuss the facts with you? Can you sit and just ask him questions? No, he stays in the center of the wheel (eye of the hurricane) and keeps everyone on the periphery"* (consciousness).

ENQUIRY—
THE NATURE OF CONSCIOUSNESS

SUMMARY

1. Trace the **I AM** back to its nature as **CONSCIOUSNESS**.

2. "See" the **I AM**ness and its reflections as made of the same **CONSCIOUSNESS**.

3. Just be "there."

CONSCIOUSNESS IS THE SUBSTANCE

Question: *In the Way of the Human Vol III: Beyond Quantum Psychology*, you have an exercise called the Chaotic swirl, where you ask what lies could **CONSCIOUSNESS** tell an observer and what lies could **CONSCIOUSNESS** tell itself. Why?

Stephen: Because **CONSCIOUSNESS** is the substance of both dual and non-dual awareness. When they say everything is **CONSCIOUSNESS,** or it is all a play of **CONSCIOUSNESS,** it means that this *mirage* of life is held together by the concept **I AM**, but it is **CONSCIOUSNESS** from which the **I AM** and this *mirage* are made. The **I AM** is a by-product of this **CONSCIOUSNESS,** so to say it is all **CONSCIOUSNESS** or a play of **CONSCIOUSNESS** is true. Everything is made of **CONSCIOUSNESS**. But it is **CONSCIOUSNESS** which makes you believe **YOU ARE** and **I AM**, and hence **CONSCIOUSNESS** makes "you" believe "you" are made of a different substance than **CONSCIOUSNESS**.

Question: So **CONSCIOUSNESS** creates the illusion?

Stephen: From **CONSCIOUSNESS** comes the concept of **I AM** and this whole world. But you are *prior* to **CONSCIOUSNESS**.

Question: Then consciousness fools us?

Stephen: Baba Prakachanda once said, **"CONSCIOUSNESS (SHAKTI) IS MAYA."**

Question: But *prior* to **CONSCIOUSNESS"** makes it seem that there is something before **CONSCIOUSNESS** which is real and different from **CONSCIOUS-NESS**.

Stephen: The Unmanifest **CONSCIOUSNESS** or **UNDIF-FERENTIATED CONSCIOUSNESS** "becomes" the manifest **CONSCIOUSNESS** and the *mirage*, but this process is only true within the *mirage* itself. Actually **NOTHING HAPPENS**. *Once CONSCIOUSNESS realizes that there is only CONSCIOUSNESS and nothing else - then there is no CONSCIOUSNESS.*

Question: So how does one discover the unmanifest?

Stephen: There really is no unmanifest. But focus your attention on **CONSCIOUSNESS** or **BEINGNESS** only. If you cannot do this, focus on the **I AM**.

Question: This sounds like what I am doing.

Stephen: Don't try to go too fast - stay where you are if you can.

Question: But why again is **CONSCIOUSNESS** the necessary substance?

Stephen: Because without it there would be no *mirage*. It is like having a gold ring and then saying, Why is the gold necessary? Worship and meditation which mean focus on, or be the **I AM** or the **CONSCIOUSNESS**.

Question: What about prayer?

Stephen: You can pray to **CONSCIOUSNESS**, or the **I AM**. But only to release "you" from its grip, not for things or so things can happen or not happen. But the one who is prayering and the one the prayering is to, are only still that same **CONSCIOUSNESS**. This is worship, this is prayer, this is devotion, and with this the **I AM** will lose its grip and you can "get" that *you are a mirage that does not know you are a mirage*. But you are not the doer, **CONSCIOUSNESS** does or does not, or, better said, gives the illusion of doing, **CONSCIOUSNESS** conceals or reveals. "You", as **I AM**, arise after the fact. Don't hate the **maya or power** of **CONSCIOUSNESS** - just be it and know what it is and **YOU ARE THAT**.

Seven

ON SPIRITUALITY
AND PRACTICE

· ·

LATER I UNDERSTOOD THE MEANING OF
SPIRITUALITY AND CAME TO THE
CONCLUSION THAT IT IS AS DISCARDABLE AS
DISHWATER. THEREFORE, I AM IN NO WAY
CONCERNED WITH SPIRITUALITY

NISARGADATTA MAHARAJ

(PG. 177, THE NECTAR OF IMMORTALITY)

SPIRITUALITY AND
THE SPIRITUAL PATH

I DO NOT ACCEPT PATHS...
ALL PATHS LEAD TO UNREALITY. PATHS ARE
CREATIONS WITHIN THE SCOPE OF KNOWLEDGE.
THEREFORE, PATHS AND MOVEMENTS CANNOT
TRANSPORT YOU INTO REALITY, BECAUSE THEIR
FUNCTION IS TO ENMESH YOU WITHIN THE
DIMENSION OF KNOWLEDGE, WHILE REALITY
PREVAILS PRIOR TO IT.

NISARGADATTA MAHARAJ
(Pg. 49, The Nectar of the Lord's Feet)

SPIRITUALITY

Nisargadatta Maharaj was quite different in his approach to spirituality. For him, the discovery and realization of **WHO YOU ARE** not only dismantles the "I" and its root the "**I AM**," but also the concept of "spirituality" and of the "path" itself.

Nisargadatta Maharaj knew that even the concept of spirituality and a path were laden with many concepts about what was "spiritual." These concepts ranged from always being loving to being a vegetarian, from sexual abstinence, to remaining silent, from worship of a deity, to the cessation of thoughts, from being forgiving to overcoming "bad" habits, and most recently from getting what you want, to improving yourself. In this way, psychology and self-help, along with spirituality, lost its direction, the discovery of **WHO YOU ARE**.

He understood that the existence of these concepts, and ideas about "spirituality" and "spiritual paths," were dependent upon the **I AM**. And, if there were no **I AM**, there could be no "spirituality" and no "spiritual path." The **I AM** is an appearance in **CONSCIOUSNESS**, an illusion, which like glue holds together the *mirage*. In "my" case, Nisargadatta used great force to smash my spiritual (path) concepts, most of which I did not even know were concepts.

With full force, one of the first things Nisargadatta Maharaj said to me was, "What spiritual knowledge have you gotten today." I replied, "What do you mean *by spiritual knowledge*." Looking back with hindsight, I can see that he was offering me an opportunity to interact and look at what "I" considered and imagined was true and spiritual so that "I" - "we" could investigate and confront its falseness. For this, I can only feel humbled with gratitude and love.

THE SUM TOTAL OF MY SPIRITUALITY NOW IS NOTHING, EVEN THAT WORD "NOTHING" IS NOT THERE, SO THERE IS NO SPIRITUALITY LEFT.

(Pg. 44, CONSCIOUSNESS And The Absolute)

Spirituality, spiritual paths, and spiritual behavior hold an infinite number of concepts ranging from Bodhisattva vows, to past lives, from Essence, to developing compassion, from non-violence and peacefulness, to unconditional love. All of these are merely "spiritual" concepts and ideals about what it means to be spiritual. These "ideas" not only have nothing to do with finding out **WHO YOU ARE**, but they actually get in the way of finding out **WHO YOU ARE**. Why? First, because you begin to believe in a non-existent self, a self that should develop qualities which are "spiritual" - but more importantly, the attempt to develop these spiritual concepts called qualities only re-enforces the "I" and the **CONSCIOUSNESS** 's reflection through the **I AM**. Furthermore, these spiritual concepts, are only true within the **I AM** *mirage*. In short, no **I AM**, no spirituality.

THE CONFRONTATION

Nisargadatta Maharaj spontaneously knew and confronted these concepts, and this *truly* was no joke. He had the ability to know and go after the most deeply-held concepts, which you might not even be aware of, confront them to "bring them on screen," and force you to look at what you did not want to look at. He held a mirror up to "my" face and showed "me" not only my spiritual concepts but my shadow side which, unknowingly, was eating away at awareness of the **I AM**.

Truly, he was not into being liked, or winning a popularity contest. "His job" was to **SMASH CONCEPTS** so that the **I AM** could be revealed, regardless of claims that he was not being spiritual, or, if he were in the Western world, of being diagnosed with some neurotic pattern. For example, one newcomer complained, "How can you be spiritual, you are sitting in a deer skin, you are not vegetarian, you seem very emotionally angry and smoke cigarettes?" Nisargadatta Maharaj replied,

YEARS AGO I LEFT MY HUMAN NATURE TO LOOK AFTER ITSELF WHAT DO I CARE?

NISARGADATTA MAHARAJ

Many people today in the year 2000 in Western Europe and the United States might feel this approach harsh or even cruel, mean, judgmental, or abusive. Its outcome, however, was unmistakable. It was difficult after the *shock* of such confrontation to ever again fully believe what you had believed before. Although some might blame the messenger—in the end, the message, like a match dropped on a haystack, caught fire and burned everything in its wake. On the first day I met Nisargadatta Maharaj "personally," the confrontation was so powerful, it was like my body were on fire. I was literally shattered and immediately I tried to rationalize a way out. For the first time in my life "I" (my ego) truly wanted to run away. Fortunately for me, though 49% of me wanted to leave, 51% kept me there until, after a short while, I couldn't get enough.

SPIRITUALITY IS NOT A CHILD'S PLAY, MY SENTENCES WILL TEAR TO PIECES . . . ANYONE WHO LISTENS TO THEM.

NISARGADATTA MAHARAJ
(Pg,. 99, CONSCIOUSNESS And The Absolute)

Nisargadatta Maharaj never let people just keep coming. He threw out many people, myself included. Nevertheless, I continued to come back, and sometimes he would let me stay, and at other times not. He had to do this because "I" was addicted to his every word. It was his words though oftentimes painful and confrontative, that forced "light bulbs to go off in my head." At first, this confrontation brought pain, but in the end only freedom. More importantly, his confrontation also validated many things that I knew were true and which concerned me about myself, or I had not fully admitted to myself that were on the periphery of my awareness. In this way, the confrontation began by battering and cracking my concepts.

WHY DOES THIS CONFLICT NORMALLY OCCUR? WHY THIS DISPUTE BETWEEN US? PEOPLE COME HERE WITH SOME PROFOUND CONCEPT OF SPIRITUAL- ITY. THEY THINK THEY HAVE SPIRI- TUAL KNOWLEDGE, AND THEY WANT ME TO GIVE THEM A CLEAN CERTIFI- CATE. "YES, YOU ARE VERY KNOWL- EDGEABLE" THIS I DON'T DO. I BLAST THEIR CONCEPTS, AND HENCE THE CONFRONTATION. . . . ALL KNOWLEDGE IS IGNORANCE.

NISARGADATTA MAHARAJ
(Pg. 392, I Am That)
(Pg. 108, Seeds Of CONSCIOUSNESS)

The Siva Sutras proclaim all bondage is caused by sound. Why? Because sound creates letters, letters creates words, words creates ideas and concepts or knowledge, which are by their nature false. The Siva Sutras say, "**KNOWLEDGE IS BONDAGE**"

It is through this type of confrontation and investigation that even the enquirer turns upon itself and evaporates like water in the sunlight. This is essential, otherwise there is a subtle belief that through enquiry, the enquir*er* is liberated and then the illusion that *"I" will then know WHO I AM*. Actually, the enquiry and enquir*er* are part of the machinery of a dualistic mind and not you. Once this is realized, enquiry ceases.

STAGES

IN THIS WAY
EVEN FAITH IN GOD IS A STAGE ALONG THE WAY.
ULTIMATELY, YOU ABANDON ALL.

(Pg. 469, I Am That)

This is often misunderstood by today's Advaita teachers. Yes, there is no "I"; however, Nisargadatta Maharaj "approach" was **ADVAITA-VEDANTA**, the realization of **THAT ONE SUBSTANCE** through negation or **NETI-NETI**, Sanskrit for **NOT-THIS-NOT-THIS**. This does indicate that there are stages which people might go through before they realize there is **NO I**.

THE GNANI IS THE BHAKTI

Once a student asked Nisargadatta Maharaj why there was no devotion or bhakti?

DEVOTION IS BHAKTI AND I AM A BHAKTI.
I AM AN ATMA BHAKTI.
I WORSHIP MYSELF (I AM).

NISARGADATTA MAHARAJ

This extraordinary statement reveals the true nature of gnani yoga and bhakti yoga. Bhakti yoga contains devotion to an outer object God, a guru, or a deity, etc., But bhakti yoga when "successful" ultimately leads to where the worship*er* and worshipp*ed*, or the lov*er* and belov*ed*, are one.

When you worship the **I AM** by being the **I AM**, bhakti is complete. The **I AM** is the deity, and when you become one with the deity or God - by being the **I AM** and negating and discarding all else - this is where bhakti meets the gnani and the lover stays faithful, "*forsaking all others*," and is the loved one - the **I AM**.

This is bhakti, this is gnani, and this is the true understanding of **ADVAITA-VEDANTA**. Advaita teachers who do not understand this mislead their students.

GIVING IT UP

WHAT YOU GAVE UP IS OF NO IMPORTANCE, WHAT HAVE YOU NOT GIVEN UP? FIND THAT OUT AND GIVE THAT UP. SADHANA IS A SEARCH FOR WHAT TO GIVE UP. EMPTY YOURSELF COMPLETELY.

NISARGADATTA MAHARA
J(Pg. 196-197, I Am That)

BEGIN TO QUESTION. THE MOST OBVIOUS THINGS ARE THE MOST DOUBTFUL. ASK YOURSELF SUCH QUESTIONS AS, WAS I REALLY BORN? AM I REALLY SO AND SO? . . . YOU HAVE PUT SO MUCH TIME INTO BUILDING A PRISON FOR YOURSELF. NOW, SPEND AS MUCH TIME ON DE-MOLISHING IT. IN FACT, DEMOLITION IS EASY, FOR THE FALSE DISSOLVES

WHEN IT IS DISCOVERED. ALL THINGS
HANG ON THE IDEA I AM. EXAMINE IT
THOROUGHLY. IT IS A SORT OF SKIN
THAT SEPARATES YOU FROM REALITY.
THE REAL IS BOTH WITHIN AND WITH-
OUT THE SKIN, BUT THE SKIN ITSELF
IS NOT REAL.

THIS I AM IDEA WAS NOT BORN WITH
YOU. YOU COULD HAVE LIVED VERY
WELL WITHOUT IT. IT CAME LATER DUE
TO YOUR SELF IDENTIFICATION WITH
THE BODY. IT CREATED THE ILLUSION
OF SEPARATION WHERE THERE IS
NONE.

NISARGADATTA MAHARAJ

(Pg. 298, I Am That)

To put together the Nisargadatta Maharaj puzzle, one must
understand that his confrontation and enquiry were just a way to
show you that upon investigation everything, including the inves-
tigator, disappears.

To "understand" Nisargadatta Maharaj, "one" must first
grasp, or *apperceive*, that when he says, *Find-out who you are* or
Who wants to know, or explore the *I AM*, or you must discover the
birth principle or child principle, or you are beyond space-time -
he is telling you that these things, called birth, death, **I AM, WHO
YOU ARE**, space-time, etc., are all imaginary, all part of the *mirage*; and, as such, they will fall away and evaporate upon investigation.

This is why, when a student asked Nisargadatta Maharaj, "**WHO ARE YOU?**" he replied, "**NOTHING PERCEIVABLE OR CONCEIVABLE.**"

His statement reveals much. It tells us that upon investigation *anything* perceivable, conceivable, or experienciable, is to be discarded. The great *mirage* of **maya** makes one believe *one is* when *one is not*. **CONSCIOUSNESS**, the substance the *mirage*, is made of "creates" the illusion of an "us" and "them," with extraordinary concepts like energy, space, mass, time, distance, location, psychology, and even spirituality. All are part of the *mirage*. Once a question was asked of Nisargadatta Maharaj, "Where did I come from?" Nisargadatta replied,

"FIND OUT HOW THIS I AM AROSE AND CAME ON YOU."

NISARGADATTA MAHARAJ

He wanted "you" to investigate so you could realize that this **I AM** did not come on you, nor is there a where; and thus these subtle, unquestioned concepts must be confronted and dismantled.

One must understand that *nothing* is, all perceivables and conceivables, including the perceiv*er* and conceiv*er*, are concepts. Concepts separate, divide, and create the illusion of a solid world with location and distance existing within the physics dimensions. Once these concepts are eliminated, the subtlety of the *mirage* of *maya* dissolves: "**YOU ARE THAT,**" Beyond this – and even "you" and beyond concepts.

GIVE UP ALL THIS TRASH, WHATEVER YOU ARE STUDYING IN THE NAME OF RELIGION, IN THE NAME OF SPIRITU-ALITY. UNDERSTAND ONLY ONE THING: THAT GODLY PRINCIPLE IS

THERE, THAT I AMNESS OR CON-
SCIOUSNESS - THAT IS THE GODLIEST
OF PRINCIPLES. IT IS THERE ONLY SO
LONG AS THE VITAL BREATH OR LIFE
FORCE IS THERE.

NISARGADATTA MAHARAJ

(PG. 177, THE ULTIMATE MEDICINE)

It is the life force which animates the breath and moves the body and the **I AM**. Stay in the **I AM**. With this simple truth, all is revealed and enquiry, in the end, falls away. Why? For two reasons: 1) It requires an enquir*er*; and 2) an enquir*ee*. Ultimately "you" understand that any enquiry. even the simplest, "**WHO AM I,**" requires, and is full of, presuppositions,

In **WHO AM I?** it supposes there is a "*who*" and an "*I*".

Any enquiry *always* presupposes that the one doing the enquiring, and what is being enquired into, are real when they are presuppositions and non-existent.

THE FIVE ELEMENTS

THERE IS NO SUCH THING AS SPIRITUALITY. WHATEVER IS, IS ONLY THIS WORLDLY LIFE IN THE FIVE-ELEMENTAL PLAY.

(PG. 44, CONSCIOUSNESS AND THE ABSOLUTE)

Maharaj always stressed that the world was a play, an interaction of the five elements of earth, air, water, fire and ether and the three forces (gunas), Tomas, Rajas and Sattva. "Spirituality," therefore, is, and can only occur, through the interaction of the five elements and forces; and they are the substratum of this "spiritual" and world illusion, which is held together by its substratum **CONSCIOUSNESS**.

It is important to understand that everything must be confronted, brought to awareness, and enquired into. At first there is a belief that if you enquire into the nature of things, the truth will be revealed. But upon that enquiry, and as you get closer to it, like a *mirage* in the desert, it vanishes. Actually there is no truth. So the purpose of enquiry is to destroy both the subject and the object of enquiry. When enquiry is turned toward the enquir*er*, it too dissolves.

As mentioned earlier, Nisargadatta knew that everything in the *mirage* was made of **CONSCIOUSNESS**. Also, as one who experientially understood Hindu tradition, he knew the basic principles of the *Bhagavad Gita*:

All is a play of the five elements, (air, earth, water, fire, and ether).

In the tradition of Hindu yoga and the *Bhagavad Gita*, Nisargadatta Maharaj continued to repeat again and again that everything occurs because of, and is subject to, the play of the elements. In this light, let's look at exploring and dismantling those concepts.

How does one begin to enquire, question, and dismantle such concepts as air, earth, water, fire and ether? Below is an enquiry which hopefully will provide a clue or hint about how to explore and dismantle this through enquiry.

ENQUIRY AS TO THE NATURE
OF THE AIR ELEMENT

Wolinsky: How does the concept of **I AM** define air?

Student: That which we all need to breathe, that which surrounds the planet.

Wolinsky: Where in the body do you feel the **I AM** concept
              and its breathing device.

Note:
The I AM is body related as are all the elements.

Student: In my lungs.

Wolinsky: Ask the **I AM** breathing device how have you de-
              ceived yourself, and allow the **I AM** to answer.

Note:
We want the I AM to answer - not its reflection.

Student: By defining myself as breathing and life.

Wolinsky: If that was just a concept of the **I AM** breathing de-
              vice, which had nothing to do with anything _____?

Student: _____Blank.

Wolinsky: If the **I AM** is separate from the breathing device,
              what occurs?

Student: Blank_____Long Silence.

Note:
**Simply un-fuse the I AM from the breathing
device so that the I AM stands alone and not
dependent, or connected to, an automatic body
process like breathing.**

Wolinsky: If the concept of **I AM** is separate from the breath-
              ing device, what does not occur?

Student: Constriction.

Wolinsky: If the **I AM** is separated from the breathing device,
              what, if anything, gets resisted?

Student: _____Blank.

Wolinsky: Regarding the air element, what must the **I AM** not know?

Student: That it isn't.

Wolinsky: If the air element was made of the same **CON-SCIOUSNESS** that the **I AM** was made of and had nothing to do with anything, _____?

Student: _____Blank.

Wolinsky: If we separate **CONSCIOUSNESS** from **I AM,** then _____?

Student: _____Silence.

Note:
Since I AM is a "derivative" or compacted or condensed CONSCIOUSNESS, the I AM must be unfused from CONSCIOUSNESS.

Wolinsky: If **I AM** is "condensed" **CONSCIOUSNESS** and you are **THAT CONSCIOUSNESS** and not the **I AM,** then. _____?

Student: _____Silence.

ENQUIRY INTO THE NATURE
OF EARTH ELEMENT

Wolinsky: Where in the body is the concept of the **I AM** that is associated with the earth element?

Student: Lower back.

Wolinsky: How does the **I AM** concept define the earth ele-
               ment?

Student: It is that which I stand on, it contains gravity, it keeps
               me grounded.

Wolinsky: If this body and earth element were a reflection of
               the **CONSCIOUSNESS** through the vehicle of the
               I AM and had nothing to do with anything,
               _____?

Student: _____Blank.

Wolinsky: What must the **CONSCIOUSNESS** which views the
               concept of the earth element through the **I AM** con-
               cept not know?

Student: That it isn't.

Wolinsky: If the concept of the earth element is part of the **I
               AM** concept and the earth element is a reflection of
               CONSCIOUSNESS and made of the same sub-
               stance as **I AM** and has nothing to do with anything,
               _____?

Student: _____Blank.

Note:

Moving deeper, we now want to separate not only
the Earth element as a reflection of the I AM, but
the I AM as a reflection of CONSCIOUSNESS.

ENQUIRY INTO THE NATURE
OF THE WATER ELEMENT

Wolinsky: Where is the concept of **I AM** that believes in the
               concept of the water element?

Student: The heart.

Wolinsky: How does the **I AM** concept define the concept of the water element?

Student: H20, it is what the body is made of.

Wolinsky: How has the **CONSCIOUSNESS** which views the concept of a water element deceived itself?

Student: That it is the **I AM** and it is me.

Wolinsky: And if this was a concept and a reflection of **CONSCIOUSNESS** through the **I AM** and had nothing to do with anything _____?

Student: _____Blank.

Wolinsky: If **CONSCIOUSNESS** is separate from the **I AM** and the water element, _____?

Student: Then I am beyond both.

Note:
Once again we are separating CONSCIOUSNESS from its primary reflection, the I AM.

Wolinsky: Is there anything that the **CONSCIOUSNESS** that "views" through the concept of **I AM** the water element must not know?

Student: It isn't.

Wolinsky: Is there anything else the **CONSCIOUSNESS** which "views" through the concept of **I AM** must not know?

Student: That it is beyond both and not it.

Wolinsky: Anything?

Student: Blank. _____. Long silence.

ENQUIRY INTO THE NATURE
OF THE FIRE ELEMENT

Wolinsky: Where is the concept of **I AM** that believes in the concept of the fire element?

Student: In the stomach.

Wolinsky: How does the concept of **I AM** define the concept of the fire element?

Student: It burns and digests food, and somehow the sun pops up like it is a sun reflection.

Wolinsky: This concept of **I AM**-fire element in your stomach, which is a sun reflection, how has it deceived itself.

Student: That "I" was it.

Wolinsky: And if the concept of **I AM** were not neither the fire elements or its sun reflection?

Student: _____Blank.

Wolinsky: What must the **CONSCIOUSNESS** which views through the concept of **I AM** not know about the fire element?

Student: That it is just **CONSCIOUSNESS.**

Wolinsky: As pure **CONSCIOUSNESS** - is it _____?

Student: _____No.

Note
Here the substance of CONSCIOUSNESS is gone
beyond as the substance that *mirage*s are made of.
Because if everything is CONSCIOUSNESS then
there is no CONSCIOUSNESS.

Wolinsky: If you separate **CONSCIOUSNESS** from **I AM** then
              _____?

Student: _____Blank as **CONSCIOUSNESS.**

Wolinsky: And if the **I AM** is separate from **CONSCIOUS-
              NESS,** and **CONSCIOUSNESS** had nothing to do
              with **I AM**?

Student: _____Peace, deep peace_____Silence.

ENQUIRY INTO THE NATURE
OF THE ETHER ELEMENT

Wolinsky: Where is the concept of **I AM** which believes in the
              concept of ether?

Student: Head.

Wolinsky: How does the **I AM** concept define the concept of
              ether?

Student: The space or the ether space that I am in.

Wolinsky: Where, in relation to the body, is the **I AM** concept,
              which believes in the concept of the ether element
              now?

Student: All around the body, and it interpenetrates through
              the body.

Wolinsky: And if the concept of the ether element were a concept of the **I AM**, which was made of **CONSCIOUS-
NESS** and had nothing to do with anything,
_____?

Student: _____Blank.

Wolinsky: If you are the **CONSCIOUSNESS** which is separate from **I AM**, then _____?

Student: **I AM** then appears in me - but I am not it.

Wolinsky: Is there such a thing as the world and **CONSCIOUS-
NESS**?

Student: No, it is like a cloud and I am the sky.

Wolinsky: And if the **CONSCIOUSNESS** cloud and sky had
nothing to do with anything, then _____?

Student: _____Long silence.

Wolinsky: And if **CONSCIOUSNESS** is separate from the
concept of **I AM** and the concept of the element of
ether, then _____?

Student: _____Blank.

Wolinsky: What must the ether element not know?

Student: That it is made of **CONSCIOUSNESS**.

Wolinsky: Why not?

Student: Then, it would not be_____Long silence?

Note:
If everything is the same substance then NOTH-
ING is.

Wolinsky: Now?

Student:

_____Blank_____**EMPTY_____NOTHINGNESS**.

SPIRITUAL PRACTICE:
BEYOND ENQUIRY

GOING BACK MEANS PRIOR TO
CONSCIOUSNESS. SO LONG AS THERE
IS A NEGATOR WHO KEEPS ON NE
GATING AND NEGATING, YOU WILL
REMAIN UN-NEGATED. IN ORDER FOR
THERE TO BE A FINAL AND TOTAL
NEGATION, THE NEGATOR HIMSELF
MUST DISAPPEAR.

NISARGADATTA MAHARAJ

Oftentimes Nisargadatta was asked, "How long does this take?" or, "Does it happen suddenly?" or, "Why practice sadhana, (spiritual practice)?" "I" asked him, "Doesn't doing a spiritual practice re-enforce an "I" doing it? And he responded:

THOSE WHO HAVE REALIZED ON THE SPOT ARE
RARE.. THE MAJORITY NEEDS SOME FORM
OF RIPENING

NISARGADATTA MAHARAJ

Question: Why does Quantum Psychology go through False-
                 Core-False Self multi-dimensional awareness if it is
                 all a *mirage*?

Wolinsky: Rarely, if ever, will the realization or *apperception*
                 that *you are not* happen suddenly. For most, *who are
                 mirages and do not know they are mirages*, there
                 seems to be stages. Quantum Psychology was a hap-
                 pening, an attempt to mark off certain stages in
                 ADVAITA-VEDANTA, certain stages *which ulti-
                 mately are not*.

Question: So there is spiritual practice?

Wolinsky: Spiritual practice is a phase, even interest, in spiri-
                 tuality; and enlightenment is a stage, a phase. Soon
                 you "see through it"; and when you do, pain ceases
                 and you get that you are a *mirage*, and that there is
                 no birth, death, beginning, or end.

Question: I know there is no I, and that spiritual practice and
                 exercises are bullshit.

Wolinsky: No you don't, you have taken on the *non-doer phi-
                 losophy*, the *no-I* philosophy because you like it and
                 it numbs out your pain. You have added a new con-
                 ceptual layer onto your old concepts.

Question: I am in pain.

Wolinsky: You used these philosophies as *medication* and a way
                 to avoid - this is bullshit - and so you suffer.

Question: My guru says I am not the doer, and exercises and
                 techniques are criminal.

Wolinsky: Your Guru misled you. You are not ready for this
                 understanding. You suffer and use this philosophy
                 to avoid and resist. When you really come to realize
                 that there is no-doer, then there is no pain. If you

have pain, then you are fooling yourself, and you have taken on spiritual philosophies and placed them on or over the "I" to numb out the pain.

YOU WILL DO A SADHANA UNTIL YOU RECEIVE THE FRUIT OF IT. EVENTU- ALLY YOU WILL RECEIVE THE RESULT IN THE PALM OF YOUR HAND. UNTIL THEN YOU WILL DO SOME PRACTICE.

NISARGADATTA MAHARAJ
(Pg. 193, The Ultimate Medicine)

Question: I don't understand (crying).

Wolinsky: You don't want to understand. You want community, you want status, friends, a spiritual life, connections, philosophical discussions, heart connections, you are not really interested in finding out **WHO YOU ARE**. When you are really interested in **THAT**, it will happen and the "I" will dissolve. For now, the "I" is solidifying and getting even stronger through your sophisticated spiritual denial mechanisms. If you are painfully lucky, when this solidifies even more, it will begin to crack.

Question: But if it is a *mirage*, am I not re-enforcing the *mirage*, by doing spiritual practice.

Wolinsky: "I" asked the same question of Nisargadatta Maharaj. He said to me, "**I don't need anything, I don't even need myself— but I still do arati (worship) to my guru everyday. This is a great mystery.**" But you don't *apperceive* it is a *mirage* and th*at you are a mirage.* Rather, these are ideas you have taken on to defend. Find out what you are defending against and give it up. As Nisargadatta Maharaj said, **YOU CAN-NOT LET GO OF SOMETHING UNTIL YOU KNOW WHAT IT IS**.

Question: Are there stages then to enlightenment?

Wolinsky: *There is no individual enlightenment.* People think there is a self that gets enlightened, like they can work hard, save and get a new house. I once had a friend who jokingly said he wanted to write a check paid to the order of Swami Muktananda 100,000 Om Namah Shivayas, as if he were buying something. Like doing mantra, being celibate, being forgiving, doing service (Karma yoga), being compassionate, being a vegetarian, etc., like you are earning a thing. This is crazy. You cannot buy your way into heaven (enlightenment) through good deeds. Like then "I" *will have something.* The "I" has an illusion that if it does something, it will get something in return. It is all a *mirage.* Find the source of this "I" which wants to "get" something. People do not understand the depth of this illusion - it includes this concept called enlightenment and the you that seeks it.

Question: It is all an illusion?

Wolinsky: A total *mirage*, you are a *mirage not knowing you are a mirage*; or, as Nisargadatta Maharaj said, **"YOU ARE THE CHILD OF A BARREN WOMAN."**

Question: In I am not the doer, something is doing the doing?

THE NON-DOER

WHEN A STAGE IS REACHED WHERE
ONE FEELS DEEPLY THAT WHATEVER IS
BEING DONE IS HAPPENING AND
ONE HAS NOT GOT ANYTHING TO DO
WITH IT, THEN IT BECOMES SUCH A
DEEP CONVICTION THAT WHATEVER IS
HAPPENING IS NOT HAPPENING RE-
ALLY. AND THAT WHATEVER SEEMS TO
BE HAPPENING IS ALSO AN ILLUSION.
THAT MAY BE FINAL. IN OTHER
WORDS, TOTALLY APART FROM WHAT-
EVER SEEMS TO BE HAPPENING,
WHEN ONE STOPS THINKING THAT
ONE IS LIVING, AND GETS THE FEEL-
ING THAT ONE IS BEING LIVED, THAT
WHATEVER ONE IS DOING, ONE IS
NOT DOING, BUT ONE IS MADE TO
DO, THEN THAT IS SORT OF A CRITE-
RION.

NISARGADATTA MAHARAJ
(Pg. 101, The Ultimate Medicine)

The I am not the doer as a concept can be dangerous if
taken on as a philosophy, because it can re-enforce the "I".

I am not the doer, enjoyer, thinker, perceiver, etc., along
with its doing, enjoying, thinking, perceiving, and done, enjoyed,
thought or perceived. Why? Because it implies subtly as though
there were a doer, thinker, perceiver, which there is *NOT*. Further-

more, it subtly implies something out there, **GOD** or **VOID**, is the **DOER**. Even the Knower of **THAT ONE SUBSTANCE** requires a separate knower to declare it is true.

As Maharaj said, **"ANYTHING YOU KNOW ABOUT YOU CANNOT BE."** Why? It implies a separate knower. The Siva Puranas say, "Those who claim to know me, know me, not. Nothing else but the **SELF (UNDIFFERENTIATED CONSCIOUSNESS)** exists."

THERE IS NO DOER

THERE IS NO DOER is a much more accurate statement. Because I am not the doer implies there is a doer like **GOD, VOID, CONSCIOUSNESS**, etc., The concept of a doer is only an appearance within the *MIRAGE*. In other words, it exists **ONLY** within the *mirage* - once you wake up from the *mirage* - "you" realize there is no doer or doing.

Simultaneously, one must understand that the machinery of doing or not doing will continue regardless of the *apperception* of **THAT**. This understanding is pivotal to understanding that the guru's or teacher's body-mind will continue to continue within the *mirage,* regardless of their *realization.*

EVEN THE PHYSICAL FORM OF THE GURU IS SUBJECT TO THE PLAY OF THE GUNAS (FORCES).

NISARGADATTA MAHARAJ

In this way, there is no way to determine "another's" attachment or non-attachment to their illusion of doing. Is "their" experience of **NOTHING**, or is "their experience," one of doing. In the former, there is **NOTHING** but *apperception* and *realization*; in the latter, there is pain.

THE BIOLOGY OF IT

To best appreciate this - everything happens spontaneously. On a biological level the concept of a doer arises after something has already occurred. The doer "I" arises after the experience has already taken place.

THINGS HAPPEN AS THEY HAPPEN. BLAME OR PRAISE ARE APPORTIONED LATER, AFTER THE SENSE OF DOERSHIP APPEARING.

NISARGADATTA MAHARAJ

(Pg. 376, I Am That)

You do not know what thought will appear two hours from now. So a thought, experience, or doing, etc., happens, and we imagine not only that there is a separate think*er* of the thought, but also that it belongs to us and is ours.

Question: In the *Way of the Human*, Vol III, you say, "Let the **VOID** do what the **VOID** does?"

Wolinsky: Yes, and it is a step before the *apperception*, that there is no doer.

Question: But it feels like *I am talking* right now.

Wolinsky: It appears that way but this appearance is in thought *only*.

Everything happens spontaneously and you imagine that there is a separate individual doer or thinker with an action. Contained within the action is the do*er* or experienc*er* of the action. Action-do*er*-experienc*er* arise spontaneously, then there is a space again. Each action has a different do*er*. Then, an "I" arises which imagines that there is only one do*er*-experienc*er* when each arises and subsides with each new experience. As does the "you" "you" think "you" are.

Question: Then, to say I am not the doer, God does, or by thy
                 will, not mine, is correct?

Wolinsky: No, it subtly implies a God who is separate from
                 you, who has a will, and performs this through you.
                 Better to realize *there is no doer-doing* because there
                 is only **ONE SUBSTANCE** or it all happens spon-
                 taneously, or contained within each doing is a sepa-
                 rate doer which arises and subsides with the action
                 itself. This will and God thing imply and contain
                 too many different substances and concepts, which
                 arise only as **CONSCIOUSNESS** reflects through
                 the **I AM,** and which do not exist independently of
                 the **CONSCIOUSNESS** or the **I AM.** The concept
                 of God having will, lessons, preferences, designs, a
                 plan, etc., is anthropomorphic because it implies God
                 has a nervous system and hence will.

                 Doing happens - there is no it doing - it's all a *mi-
                 rage.* You are a *mirage.* If you were thirsty and saw
                 water in the desert and tried to drink it, would your
                 thirst be quenched? You suffer, and so you go after
                 spirituality like a thirsty person goes after water in a
                 mirage in the desert. After years of drinking out of
                 this *mirage*, you still suffer. Why? *Because not only
                 is the water of spirituality a mirage - but you are a
                 mirage.*

                 There is no doer or doing is a cleaner way of ex-
                 pressing rather than I am not the doer which implies
                 a doer. There is only this space-time *mirage* which
                 you appear to be. This you cannot *apperceive* be-
                 cause you have not "gotten" you are a *mirage.*

                 When you sleep at night, you dream you went to
                 Hawaii, fought a tiger, did whatever, then, when you
                 awake this "you" is gone - it was a *mirage.* Do you
                 feel bad because the dream character is no more.

ONE SUBSTANCE

Question: You do say that there is only one substance?

Wolinsky: Yes, from the illusionary **I AM** or **NOT-I-I.** However, when the "I" disappears, there is not even one **SUBSTANCE, CONSCIOUSNESS, EMPTINESS, A VOID** or awareness or even Beyond because there is no awar*er* or know*er* or anything to say it is so. There is no **VOID, BEYOND** or **ENLIGHTENMENT** because there is **NO-I** to say it is so.

Question: Why did you say, and I quote "enlightenment is the realization that there is only one substance?"

Wolinsky: I said that is the only thing you could say, "after this," Nothing can be said. Because soon you realize that even the know*er* or perceiv*er* of the **ONE-SUBSTANCE** is part of the *mirage* and is a concept.

Question: In the *Way of the Human*, you say liberation is a concept - others say it is a reality, can you say something about this.

Wolinsky: From the "point of view" of the absolute - liberation is a concept - from the point of view of the body-mind lens - it is an idea. From the point of view of pure **I AM** - the concept of liberation and bondage are both concepts of the **I AM** and exist only within the *mirage*. From the "point of view of **CONSCIOUSNESS**, there is only **CONSCIOUSNESS**." In other words, the *mirage* character now thinks there is bondage or liberation - but the *mirage* person is NOT. Don't be deceived by the **I AM** thing. It is "your" touchstone between manifest and unmanifest - but also if you believe in it and what manifests out of it - it will be your nemesis.

Question: In the *Way of the Human*, you talk about **THAT ONE
                 SUBSTANCE**. Is that the same as Nisargadatta
                 Maharaj's **I AM THAT**?

Wolinsky: Let us start off by saying that there are two levels of
                 I AM - the verbal **I AM**, which Nisargadatta Maharaj
                 said, "All I can *say* is **I AM**." And the non-verbal **I
                 AM**, which is no thoughts, memory, emotions, as-
                 sociations perceptions, attention, or intentions. This
                 non-verbal **I AM** is the seed of your universe and is
                 part of the body. No body-no **I AM**.

        Then, there is the **BEINGNESS** of pure **CONSCIOUS-
NESS**, which is when the non-verbal **I AM** evaporates and there is
no longer an **I AM**. Hence, you *apperceive* a **BEINGNESS**, which
is awareness with **NOTHING** to be aware of. Soon the awarer
merges and there is only **THAT ONE SUBSTANCE**. **I AM THAT**
is beyond **I AM THAT ONE SUBSTANCE**. **THAT** is the only
word used to describe it. You could say it is beyond, but beyond
implies a place or location. You could say it is the unmanifest *prior*
to manifest beingness or **ONE SUBSTANCE**, but that implies a
prior as in time. Just realize that **WHATEVER YOU SAY IT IS -
IT IS NOT**.

Question: Jung and others believe thirst dreams have mean-
                 ing.

Wolinsky: Dreams are *mirage*s within the *mirage*. If you want
                 the *mirage* person you think you are to find out **WHO
                 YOU ARE**, it means evaporation, give up looking
                 for meanings in the dream or waking state. But know
                 there is no finding out **WHO YOU ARE**. It is like
                 you are a person in a dream who is in Hawaii. When
                 you awake from the dream, the Hawaii person is gone
                 - so too, *when you awake, there is no-you*.

Question: But doesn't **CONSCIOUSNESS** do?

Wolinsky: **CONSCIOUSNESS** is there only as long as the body is there. **CONSCIOUSNESS** is what the dream *mirage* is made of, the *mirage* is an appearance.

Question: But you say everything is the **VOID** of **UNDIFFER-ENTIATED CONSCIOUSNESS**?

Wolinsky: Yes, it was a way of saying everything is **ONE SUB-STANCE**; but, if you read deeper into the last sentence of the book *Quantum Consciousness*, it says, *"There is no quantum "consciousness" because there would have to a separate "I" to say it was so - so Quantum Consciousness leaves you here and so do I."*

Question: Even **CONSCIOUSNESS** is part of the *mirage*?

Wolinsky: Yes, this is why Nisargadatta Maharaj called his book *Prior to Consciousness* it was a way to point to that direction.

Question: Yet there are stages?

Wolinsky: In the dream-*mirage* there seems to be - don't push it, just let it happen. don't try to make it happen. People take on these spiritual philosophies too early, so they suffer more. Nisargadatta Maharaj gave each disciple what they needed - he even gave them mantras.

Question: Did it serve a purpose?

Wolinsky: In the *mirage* there is no purpose, only the illusion of purpose. We are all dream characters in a *mirage*, with neither beginning nor end.

ON MEDITATION
AND SPIRITUAL PRACTICE

THE WORSHIPER IS IN THE CONSCIOUSNESS, AND THE OBJECT OF WORSHIP IS ALSO CONSCIOUSNESS.

NISARGADATTA MAHARAJ
(Consciousness and the Absolute)

CONSCIOUNESS is the substance that the mirage is made of. To call it the *play of CONSCIOUSNESS* clearly says it all. But what does that mean? That can best be summed up by the following statement of Baba Prakashanada, that "Shaki (**CONSCIOUSNESS**) is maya." This statement reveals a simple but profound truth, that **CONSCIOUSNESS** is the substance of the *mirage* - but also that **CONSCIOUSNESS** itself plays a part called "you" and a part called "me". It plays the part of **I AM** and it is the substance the **I AM** is made of. You could say that **CONSCIOUSNESS** is the **I AM** and it is the substance the **I AM** is made of. You could say that the **I AM** is a by-product of **CONSCIOUSNESS** and that **CONSCIOUSNESS** is "prior" to **I AM**.

Question: What then are all the meditation practices?

Wolinsky: The experience of mantra (sound), yantra (light), or
                tantra (expansion of knowledge) originally were
                spontaneous happenings, spontaneous "experiences"
                which occurred when **CONSCIOUSNESS** through
                the **I AM** turned within or back on itself. Going or
                turning within is when the reflection turns within or
                goes within and *apperceives* its source (**I AM**) and
                the **CONSCIOUSNESS**, and "remains" there.

                Unfortunately, when these "spontaneous experi-
                ences," or happenings, are reported to others, these
                others ("I"s) imagine that if they duplicate the spon-

taneous happening by doing practice, (i.e., repeating a mantra, focusing on a vision or yantra or tantra action, etc.), then **IT**, the disappearance, will happen to them as well as to "others." Notice that this rarely, if ever, occurs. Why? Because, **THE "I" DOING THE MEDITATION AND WANTING TO GET SOMETHING, IS A REFLECTION OF THE CONSCIOUSNESS** through the **I AM.** The "I" believes it is doing it and it can bring about "this happening" (no "I") and it (the "I") will get something. Rather than the **I AM** just being itself whereby these "spiritual" happenings occur.

The problem is that the "I" seeking its own self-destruction is trying to create a state to enhance its belief that **IT IS** so it can *have and get something* and survive better imaging that it can control **THAT.** The "I" does not realize that there is *NO-I*, and that **CONSCIOUSNESS** either reveals or conceals itself, regardless of what an "I" does or does not do.

THERE IS NOTHING YOU CAN DO TO SLOW IT DOWN, NOTHING YOU CAN DO TO SPEED IT UP.

NISARGADATTA MAHARAJ

Question: You seem so critical of meditation, and yet Maharaj tells people to meditate?

Wolinsky: What form of meditation are you thinking about? Mantras, yantras, and tantras can help to teach someone to focus the mind or even become more relaxed. But oftentimes they are used to create a state. In this way, *a false self I-dentity is doing the technique, to get something which enhances its survival and belief that it is. Who meditates is the question.*

WHAT I MEAN BY MEDITATION IS TO REJECT ALL EXPERIENCE AND BE IN THE EXPERIENCELESS STATE.

(Pg. 194, Seeds of consciousness)

The non-verbal **I AM** is the gateway or portal to **CONSCIOUSNESS** and **THAT**. If one stays in no thoughts, memory, emotions, associations, perceptions, attention, or intentions, that is the **I AM**. Meditation is just to **BE**, not to do. Maharaj was into meditation but only as a way to focus on the **I AM**, *stay there*, *discard* anything that arises that is not the **I AM**, and trace and find the source of the **I AM** which is **CONSCIOUSNESS**. In short, to just **BE. THEN THE MEDITATOR BECOMES THE OBJECT OF MEDITATION**

Maharaj was not into using techniques to create a state, though he suggested that for beginners, a mantra might be a step. We understood, however, that for it to be a step, the mantra, the repeater of the mantra, and the mantra itself, must be the same - then the **I AM** is realized. Maharaj "wanted you" to find the **I AM** and ultimately to go beyond it (for it to evaporate). If you stay in the **I AM**, discard all else, and trace everything back to the source of the **I AM**, you go into the **NOTHINGNESS**.

This he called **ADVAITA** (non-dual) awareness and this was his meditation.

WHEN THE DHYANA-YOGA IS DONE CORRECTLY BEINGNESS DISSOLVES GRADUALLY INTO NON·BEINGNESS.

NISARGADATTA MAHARAJ

(PG. 24, THE NECTAR OF IMMORTALITY)

Question: You seem to be critical of meditation, and yet in
               Hearts on Fire there are many meditations, Why?

Wolinsky: I am not critical of meditation. I am concerned when
               *meditation is being used as medication, or when it
               is being done by an "I" to get something or survive
               better*. For example, someone feels anger or fear, etc.,
               and they adopt a "spiritual" philosophy to support
               doing some form of meditation or "psychological
               reframe" to *get rid* of these emotions. In this way,
               these emotions are labeled as bad. When this occurs,
               it is a False Self Identity which is trying to get rid of
               an emotion. It is attempting to create a state. Once
               the meditation is over, the state, as with all states,
               disappears. And a new state and a new identity, which
               either loves or hates the state, arises. It is a never-
               ending cycle, laden with judgments about states.

Question: But you and others, even Nisargadatta Maharaj, of-
               fer many meditations.

Wolinsky: Yes, and unfortunately, as I have seen with Rajaneesh
               (OSHO) disciples, even sexual meditations were
               merely newly-created spiritual identities which were
               placed on top of other more rigid character struc-
               tures which ultimately only supported, hid and re-
               enforced the deeper structures. *"Spiritual I-
               dentities," as Yogananda Paramahansa said, "are
               the most difficult to get rid of."*

Question: But you offer them still?

Wolinsky: That is true, to get people to focus and discard what
               is not them—not to create a state. Think of it this
               way. Hundreds of years ago, a Tibetan lama would
               sit in meditation, a vision would spontaneously ap-
               pear before him which he would paint, hence yantras
               or thangkas. Today, there are shops which manufac-
               ture and sell these paintings.

Meditations, like seeing lights, etc., are reflections of the **CONSCIOUSNESS** through the **I AM** which arose spontaneously. Later, the reflections were made into techniques and the **CONSCIOUSNESS** and the **I AM,** the reflector of these experiences, was forgotten. In other words, you forgot yourself, the **I AM**. Meditation should be natural (**NISARGA**).

Now, people have experiences and get hooked on them; worse yet, *they decide the experiences mean something*. I was once with Baba Prakashanada and I asked him about *his* spiritual experiences. He said,

IF I TELL YOU MY EXPERIENCES, I'LL THINK I HAD THEM— EXPERIENCES ARE EGO.

All experiences must have an experienc*er*, they occur within phenomena only. However, in the very beginning, you imagine "you" are meditating. If that happens, let it happen. It will fall away as the I-dentity who imagines it is meditating falls away.

THE MEDITATOR IS PRIOR TO THE MEDITATION.

NISARGATTA MAHARAJ
(Pg. 115, Seeds Of CONSCIOUSNESS)

What is meditation? Classically meditation is the focusing of attention on a fixed object or space. It is also called the uninterrupted flow of attention, like oil being poured from one container into another. What did Maharaj mean by meditation, stay in the **I**

AM, and discard all else? This is *pure* bhakti whereby the object of devotion (or loved one), and the devotee (the lover) are one, and all else is to be discarded. We call it pure because there is no subject-object. This is **NISARGA YOGA** or Natural Yoga.

Maharaj began with the outermost levels to be gone beyond and worked inward, discarding subtler and subtler concepts, until the verbal **I AM**, the Non Verbal **I AM** and even the **WITNESS** were gone beyond (evaporated). This, for Nisargadatta Maharaj, was an on-going process not limited to a meditation room, ashram, retreat center, or study group.

MEDITATION IS A DELIBERATE ATTEMPT TO PIERCE INTO THE HIGHER STATES OF CONSCIOUSNESS AND FINALLY GO BEYOND IT. THE ART OF MEDITATION IS THE ART OF SHIFTING THE FOCUS OF ATTENTION TO EVER SUBTLER LEVELS, WITHOUT LOSING ONE'S GRIP ON THE LEVELS LEFT BEHIND. IN A WAY, IT IS LIKE HAVING DEATH UNDER CONTROL. ONE BEGINS WITH THE LOWEST LEVELS: SOCIAL CIRCUMSTANCES, CUSTOMS AND HABITS, THEIR PHYSICAL SURROUNDINGS, THE POSTURE AND THE BREATHING OF THE BODY, THE SENSES, THEIR SENSATIONS AND PERCEPTIONS, THE MIND, ITS THOUGHTS AND FEELINGS - UNTIL THE ENTIRE MECHANISM OF PERSONALITY IS GRASPED AND FIRMLY HELD. THE FINAL STAGE OF MEDITATION IS

REACHED WHEN THE SENSE OF IDEN-
TITY GOES BEYOND THE 'I-AM-SO-
AND-SO', BEYOND 'SO-I-AM', BEYOND
'I-AM-THE-WITNESS-ONLY'. BEYOND
'THERE-IS', BEYOND ALL IDEAS, INTO
THE IMPERSONALLY PERSONAL PURE
BEING. BUT YOU MUST BE ENER-
GETIC WHEN YOU TAKE TO MEDITA-
TION. IT IS DEFINITELY NOT A PART-
TIME OCCUPATION. LIMIT YOUR IN-
TERESTS AND ACTIVITIES TO WHAT IS
NEEDED FOR YOU AND YOUR DEPEN-
DENTS' BAREST NEEDS. SAVE ALL
YOUR ENERGIES AND TIME FOR
BREAKING THE WALL YOUR MIND HAS
BUILT AROUND YOU. BELIEVE ME,
YOU WILL NOT REGRET IT.

NISARGADATTA MAHARAJ
(PG. 412-413, I AM THAT)

BEYOND SPACE-TIME

To discover who you are by discovering who you are not is to go beyond not only psychology but ultimately also **CONSCIOUSNESS** itself. One of the important *realizations* in Quantum Psychology occurs when "we" take the label off and having any reflection, i.e. thought, emotion, image, etc., as **CONSCIOUSNESS,** and then *apperceive* the delabeler as **CONSCIOUSNESS.**

Question: Nisargadatta Maharaj says all, including space and time are concepts. How can this be?

Wolinsky: Let's go back to a beginning process in Quantum
              Psychology. Notice an emotion.

Question: Okay

Wolinsky: Notice where in the body you feel the emotion

Question: Okay

Wolinsky: Take the label off and have it as energy

Question: Nods.

Wolinsky: Now, take the label of energy off and dive into the
              EMPTINESS below the energy label. What's go-
              ing on?

Question: **JUST PURE NOTHINGNESS.**

Wolinsky: If the "I" that is experiencing the **NOTHINGNESS**
              is made of the same substance as the **NOTHING-
              NESS** then _____?

Question: _____Long silence.

Note:
The **NOTHINGNESS** of No-I is pure **UNDIF-
FERENTIATED CONSCIOUSNESS** or the
**VOID OF UNDIFFERENTIATED CON-
SCIOUSNESS**.

SPIRITUAL EXPERIENCES:
THE GREAT ILLUSION

We begin by understanding that to "Realize" is to *apperceive* that there is no self, and, more importantly, that all states of
CONSCIOUSNESS - high, low, good, bad, or indifferent - are
still states made of **CONSCIOUSNESS**, no more no less. When
asked if *he* was in samadhi Maharaj replied,

SAMDHI IS A STATE,
I AM NOT IN A STATE

In this way, *all* states are in **CONSCIOUSNESS** and are all only *mirage* based. It was the stateless state of **I AM** or the No-State state prior to the concept of "spirituality" itself which Nisargadatta was pointing toward.

When I was with Baba Prakashananda in 1977, I once told him I wanted Moksha (Sanskrit for liberation), and he asked me, "What is Moksha?" I responded with ONENESS, BLISS, etc., As I told him what I thought it was, "I" *apperceived* clearly that all I said was bullshit. As "I" watched this bullshit come out of "my" mouth, it was obvious that they were just concepts and they disappeared.

SPIRITUAL WAY STATIONS

ESSENCE - I AM - COLLECTIVE -
VOID AND THE NAMELESS ABSOLUTE AS =
SPIRITUAL ILLUSIONS

As mentioned earlier, as with all illusions, the spiritual illusions, according to Yogananda Paramahansa, are the most difficult to give up. Why? According to Nisargadatta Maharaj, it is because they go unquestioned. Certainly the nature and existence of such "spiritual" states and concepts as **ESSENCE - I AM - COLLECTIVE - VOID - NAMELESS ABSOLUTE - BEYOND** and **MULTI-DIMENSIONAL AWARENESS** are not in question. However, they are way stations and that is all. Thus, they all need to be dismantled.

ENQUIRY

Enquiry into the Nature of Essence: An Overview

1. What concept does the concept of **I AM** have about the concept of *Essence*?

  2.   Why would the concept of **I AM** come up with that concept?

  3.   If that concept had nothing to with anything, then. . . ?

AN ENQUIRY DEMONSTRATION INTO THE NATURE OF ESSENCE

Wolinsky: What concept does the concept of **I AM** have about the concept of Essence?

Student: That essence is this peaceful loving space.

Wolinsky: Why would the concept of **I AM** come up with that concept?

Student: Because that's what it is supposed to be.

Wolinsky: If that was just a concept of the **I AM** and had nothing to do with anything, then. . . ?

Student: _____Blank.

Wolinsky: What other concepts does the concept of **I AM** have about the concept of Essence?

Student: It is important, better, higher, significant.

Wolinsky: Why would the concept of **I AM** come up with that concept?

Student: That's what it was told.

Wolinsky: It was told or it told itself?

Student: Well, it thinks it came from outside.

Wolinsky: If it came from itself and its own reflection then. . . ?

Student: _____Silence.

Wolinsky: If essence was just a concept of the **I AM** and had
              nothing to do with anything, then. . . ?

Student: _____Blank

Wolinsky: What other concepts does the concept of **I AM** have
              about the concept of Essence?

Student: _____Big empty vastness.

Wolinsky: Why would the concept of **I AM** come with that
              concept?

Student: That's what the experience is.

Wolinsky: If the experienc*er* of the vastness and the experi-
              ence or vastness are made of the same **CON-
              SCIOUSNESS**, then _____?

Student: _____**NOTHINGNESS**.

Wolinsky: If vastness was just a concept of **I AM** and had noth-
              ing to do with anything, then. . . ?

Student: _____**NOTHINGNESS**.

Wolinsky: Any other concepts that the concept of **I AM** has
              about the concept of Essence?

Student: _____Blank_____
              Just blank _____**NOTHINGNESS**.

ENQUIRY

Into the nature of I AM: An Overview.

1. What concept does the concept of **I AM** have about the concept of the **I AM**

2. Why would the concept of **I AM** come up with that concept?

3. If that concept had nothing to do with anything, then. . . ?

AN ENQUIRY DEMONSTRATON
INTO THE NATURE OF I AM

Wolinsky: What concept does the concept of **I AM** have about the concept of the **I AM**?

Student: That it is.

Wolinsky: Why would the concept of **I AM** come with the concept of **IS**?

Student: Because it believes it is.

Wolinsky: If the concept of **IS** was just a concept of **I AM** which had nothing to do with anything, then. . . ?

Student: _____Blank_____Silence.

Wolinsky: What other concept does the concept of **I AM** have about the concept of the **I AM**?

Student: That it's a gateway and important.

Wolinsky: Why would the concept of **I AM** come up with that concept?

Student: That's what it was told.

Wolinsky: If the **I AM** told itself that but it appeared to come
                from outside and it had nothing to do with anything
                then _____?

Student: _____Blank.

Wolinsky: If all of these concepts had nothing to do with any-
                thing, then. . . ?

Student: _____Blank.

Wolinsky: What other concept does the concept of **I AM** have
                about the concept of **I AM?**

Student: It is presence.

Wolinsky: Why would the concept of **I AM** come up with the
                concept of presence?

Student: That is its experience.

Wolinsky: If the experienc*er* of that concept called presence,
                and the experience or presence were both made of
                the same **CONSCIOUSNESS** then. . . ?

Student: _____Blank.

Wolinsky: If all of these concepts had nothing to do with any-
                thing, then. . . ?

Student: _____Blank.

Wolinsky: What other concepts does the concept of **I AM** have
                about the concept of **I AM?**

Student: _____Blank.

Wolinsky: Are there any other concepts that the concept of **I AM** has about the concept of the **I AM**?

Student: That it's a concept.

Wolinsky: Why would the concept of **I AM** come up with the concept of a concept?

Student: I don't know.

Wolinsky: If that knowing or not knowing were just concepts of **CONSCIOUSNESS** "through" the **I AM** and had nothing to do with anything, then. . . ?

Student: _____Blank _____**NOTHING**.

Wolinsky: Tell me a concept that the concept of **I AM** has about the concept of the **I AM**?

Student: _____**NOTHING** _____Blank.

ENQUIRY

In the Nature of Collective: An Overview

1. What concepts does the concept of **I AM** have about the concept of **COLLECTIVE**?

2. Why would the concept of **I AM** come up with that concept?

3. If that concept had nothing to with anything, then. . . ?

AN ENQUIRY DEMONSTRATION
INTO THE NATURE OF THE COLLECTIVE

Wolinsky: What concept does the concept of **I AM** have about the concept of **COLLECTIVE**?

Student: That it contains archetypes and a **CONSCIOUS-NESS** which connects everything.

Wolinsky: Why would the concept of **I AM** come up with the concept of Archetypes and **CONSCIOUSNESS** which connects everything?

Student: It was its experience.

Wolinsky: If the experiencer of this and the experience were made of the same **CONSCIOUSNESS** then. . . ?

Student: _____Blank.

Wolinsky: If these concepts had nothing to do with anything, then. . . ?

Student: _____Blank.

Wolinsky: What other concepts does the concept of **I AM** have about the concept of **COLLECTIVE**?

Student: That it rules everything.

Wolinsky: Why would the concept of **I AM** come up with that concept?

Student: Because that's what it was told.

Wolinsky: If what it was told was the **I AM** concept telling it to itself then. . . ?

Student: _____Blank. It becomes **NOTHINGNESS**
                      again_____.

Wolinsky: If these concepts of the **I AM** had nothing to do with
              anything, then. . . ?

Student: _____Blank.

Wolinsky: What other concept does the concept of **I AM** have
              about the concept of the **COLLECTIVE**?

Student: _____None.

Wolinsky: Anything?

Student: _____Blank_____Spacey_____Gone.

ENQUIRY

Into the Nature of the Void: An Overview

1. What concept does the concept of **I AM** have
    about the concept of the **VOID**?

2. Why would the concept of **I AM** come up with
    that concept?

3. If that concept had nothing to with anything,
    then. . . ?

AN ENQUIRY DEMONSTRATION INTO THE NATURE OF VOID

Wolinsky: What concept does the concept of **I AM** have about
              the concept of **VOID**?

Student: That it's empty.

Wolinsky: Why would the concept of **I AM** come up with the concept of empty?

Student: That is its experience.

Wolinsky: If the experience of empty and the experiencer of empty are made of the same **CONSCIOUSNESS**, then. . . ?

Student: _____Long Silence.

Wolinsky: If these concepts of VOID and Empty had nothing to do with anything, then. . . ?

Student: _____Long Silence.

Wolinsky: What other concept does the concept of **I AM** have about the concept of **VOID**?

Student: It's dark and round.

Wolinsky: Why would the concept of **I AM** come with the concept of dark and round?

Student: That is its experience.

Wolinsky: If the experien*cer* of dark and round and the experience of dark and round were both are made of the same **CONSCIOUSNESS**, then_____?

Student: _____Blank_____**NOTHINGNESS.**

Wolinsky: If these concepts of the **I AM** had nothing to do with anything, then. . . ?

Student: _____Silence.

Wolinsky: What other concept does the concept of **I AM** have about the concept of **VOID**?

Student: It's surrounded by the **NAMELESS ABSOLUTE**.

Wolinsky: Why would the concept of **I AM** come up with that
                 concept?

Student: That is its experience.

Wolinsky: And if the experiencer and experience of this are
                 made of the same **CONSCIOUSNESS**, then...?

Student: _____Silence.

Wolinsky: If all of these concepts had nothing to do with any-
                 thing, then. . . . ?

Student: _____Blank_____Silence.

Wolinsky: What other concept does the concept of **I AM** have
                 about the concept of **VOID**?

Student: That it is **IT**.

Wolinsky: Why would the concept of **I AM** come with the con-
                 cept of **IT**?

Student: The **I AM** assumes that if it experiences something,
                 that it is real and it is.

Wolinsky: If the concept of *real* and *is* that the concept of **I AM**
                 came up with had nothing to do with anything,
                 then...?

Student: _____Blank_____Silence.

Wolinsky: What other concept does the concept of **I AM** have
                 about the concept of **VOID**?

Student: Nothing is.

Wolinsky: Why would the concept of **I AM** come up with that concept?

Student: Because that is its experience.

Wolinsky: If all of these concepts had nothing to do with anything, then...?

Student: Then, there is no **NOTHING**_____Silence.

Wolinsky: Any other concept that the concept of **I AM** has about the concept of **VOID**?

Student: _____No_____Long silence.

Wolinsky: Anything?

Student: _____ Silence.

THE NAMELESS ABSOLUTE

There is not one **VOID**, but an infinite number of **VOID** universes. It is futile to worship one god or goddess within any one **VOID** universe. Rather, notice, that the **VOID** universes and the Gods and Goddesses can only be as long as the **I AM** is there. By turning full attention around on the **I AM,** staying with it, and discarding all else – **THAT** is *apperceived.* This is the message of Nisargadatta Maharaj.

THERE ARE INNUMERABLE GODS, EACH WITHIN HIS OWN UNIVERSE.

NISARGADATTA MAHARAJ

(Pg. 440, I Am That)

ENQUIRY

Into the Nature of the Nameless Absolute: An Overview

1. What concepts does the concept of **I AM** have about the concept of the *NAMELESS ABSO-LUTE*?

2. Why would the concept of **I AM** come up with that concept?

3. If that concept had nothing to with anything, then. . . ?

ENQUIRY INTO THE NATURE OF THE NAMELESS ABSOLUTE

Wolinsky: What concept does the concept of **I AM** have about the concept of the **NAMELESS ABSOLUTE**?

Student: That it surpasses the **VOID**, that the **VOIDs** are like holes in the **NAMELESS ABSOLUTE**.

Wolinsky: Why would the concept of **I AM** come up with that concept?

Student: It is its idea.

Wolinsky: If all of these concepts had nothing to do with anything, then...?

Student: _____Wow_____!

Wolinsky: What other concepts does the concept of **I AM** have about the concept of **NAMELESS ABSOLUTE**?

Student: It is just a name for something.

Wolinsky: Why would the **I AM** come up with the concept of having to name things?

Student: Makes it feel like it is.

Wolinsky: And if **IT IS** and naming were just part of the **I AM** and had nothing to do with anything, then. . . ?

Student: _____Blank_____Silence.

Wolinsky: What other concepts does the concept of **I AM** have about the concept of the **NAMELESS ABSOLUTE**?

Student: There isn't anything.

Wolinsky: Why would the concept of **I AM** come up with that concept?

Student: I don't know.

Wolinsky: If that concept had nothing to do with anything, then...?

Student: _____Blank_____Silence.

Wolinsky: What other concepts does the concept of **I AM** have about the concept of the **NAMELESS ABSOLUTE**?

Student: None_____Long silence.

ENQUIRY

Into the Nature of Beyond: An Overview

1.   What concepts does the concept of **I AM** have about the concept of *BEYOND*?

2. Why would the concept of **I AM** come up with that concept?

3. If that concept had nothing to with anything, then. . . ?

AN ENQUIRY DEMONSTRATION INTO THE NATURE OF BEYOND

Wolinsky: What concept does the concept of **I AM** have about the concept of **BEYOND**?

Student: That it exists someplace.

Wolinsky: Why would the concept of **I AM** come up with that concept?

Student: It is an idea and a reflection of **I AM.**

Wolinsky: If that concept had nothing to do with anything, then..?

Student: _____ ___Space_____Blank.

Wolinsky: What other concept does the concept of **I AM** have about the concept of **BEYOND**?

Student: It's like my heaven, it takes care of everything.

Wolinsky: Why would the concept of **I AM** come up with that concept?

Student: It is a reflection of **CONSCIOUSNESS.**

Wolinsky: If these were just concepts that had nothing to do with anything, then...?

Student: I feel a little let down that there is no **BEYOND.**

Wolinsky: If the concept of let-down and Beyond and the experiencer of let-down and beyond were just concepts which were all made of the same substance or **CONSCIOUSNESS** and had nothing to with anything, then. . . ?

Student: Wow! I don't know what I am.

Wolinsky: What other concept does the **CONSCIOUSNESS** through the concept of **I AM** have about the concept of **BEYOND**?

Student: That it's a maze and it exists.

Wolinsky: Why would the **CONSCIOUSNESS** through the concept of **I AM** come with that concept?

Student: I don't know. _____**NOTHING.**

Wolinsky: If these concepts had nothing to do with anything, then. . . ?

Student: _____Blank____Silence_____**NOTHINGNESS.**

Wolinsky: Any other concepts that the concept of **I AM** has about the concept of **BEYOND**?

Student: _____Just quiet_____Long silence.

ENQUIRY

*In the Nature of Multi Dimensional Awareness:
An Overview*

1.   What concept does the concept of **I AM** have about the concept of **MULTI-DIMEN-SIONAL AWARENESS**?

2.   Why would the concept of **I AM** come up with that concept?

3.   If that concept had nothing to with anything, then. . . ?

AN ENQUIRY DEMONSTRATION INTO THE NATURE OF MULTI-DIMENSIONAL AWARENESS

Wolinsky: What concept does the concept of **I AM** have about the concept of **MULTI-DIMENSIONAL AWARE-NESS**?

Student: That it's important.

Wolinsky: Why would the concept of **I AM** come up with that concept?

Student: It is a nice **I AM** reflection.

Wolinsky: Why would the concept of **I AM** come with that concept?

Student: It makes it more real, like **IT IS**.

Wolinsky: And if the concept of **IS** was just a concept of the concept of **I AM** and had nothing to do with anything, then. . . ?

Student: Blank_____Silence.

Wolinsky: What other concept does the concept of **I AM** have about the concept of **MULTI DIMENSIONAL AWARENESS**?

Student: It aids in enlightenment.

Wolinsky: Why would the concept of **I AM** come with that concept?

Student: Makes sense.

Wolinsky: If the concept called "Makes sense" and enlightenment were just concepts of the concept of **I AM** and had nothing to do with anything, then. . . . ?

Student: _____Blank_____Long silence.

Wolinsky: What other concepts does the concept of **I AM** have about the concept of **MULTI DIMENSIONAL AWARENESS**?

Student: That it likes it because *it gets to do* something.

Wolinsky: Why would the concept of **I AM** come up with that concept of *liking to do something*?

Student: I don't know.

Wolinsky: If all of these were concepts that had nothing to do with anything, then...?

Student: _____Blank_____ Long silence.

Wolinsky: What other concept does the concept of **I AM** have about the concept of **MULTI DIMENSIONAL AWARENESS**?

Student: That they exist.

Wolinsky: Why would the concept of **I AM** come up with that concept?

Student: I don't know.

Wolinsky: If it were just a concept of the **I AM** and had nothing to do with anything, then. . . . ?

Student: _____Silence.

Stephen;   What other concepts does the concept of **I AM** have about the concept of **MULTI-DIMENSIONAL AWARENESS**?

Student: That the **CONSCIOUSNESS** reflects out **I AM** and forgets it does that and believes its reflection.

Wolinsky: Why would the **CONSCIOUSNESS** through the concept of **I AM** come with that concept?

Student: It does.

Wolinsky: If these were just concepts and had nothing do to with anything, then. . . ?

Student: _____Silence.

Wolinsky: Any other concepts that the concept of **I AM** has about the concept of **MULTI-DIMENSIONAL AWARENESS**?

Student: Who gives a shit what the **CONSCIOUSNESS** or the **I AM** reflects out?

Wolinsky: Why would the concept of **I AM** come with that concept?

Student: Who gives a shit?

Wolinsky: If that concept of giving or not giving a shit had nothing to with anything, then. . . ?

Student: _____Silence.

SPIRITUALITY:
AN INTERESTING IDEA

Perhaps, "spiritual" concepts and practices are very difficult things to look at and discard. Possibly because other psycho-emotional concepts are more painful, that we are more apt to work with them, whereas spiritual concepts "promise" us relief from the pain. Unfortunately, as we all know, spiritual concepts may help to numb the pain, offer a nicer frame of reference or lens - but even after years, the subtle pain remains, as we try, with spiritual philosophies, communities, and techniques, to justify the stuckness ignoring the *understructure* by not questioning "spiritual" concepts themselves and how they hook into our *understructures*. This ultimately re-enforces the **CONSCIOUSNESS** reflected concept of psychology and the concept of spirituality through the **I AM** thus keeping the entire cycle going. To paraphrase and combine several statements made by Nisargatta Maharaj,

DISCARD ALL. . .
YOU CANNOT LET-GO OF
SOMETHING UNTIL YOU KNOW WHAT IT IS. . .
LIKE A MAN DIGGING A WELL, DO NOT STOP
DIGGING UNTIL YOU HIT WATER. . .
DISCARD ALL UNTIL ALL THAT
IS LEFT IS NOTHING. . .
BELIEVE ME THERE CANNOT BE TOO
MUCH DESTRUCTION

NISARGADATTA MAHARAJ

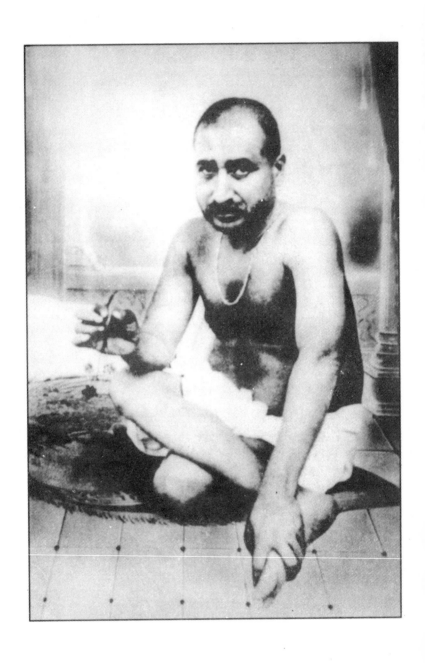

SRI SIDDHARAMESHWAR MAHARAJ

NISARGADATTA MAHARAJ'S GURU

Eight

THE GURU

. . . .

YOUR OWN SELF IS THE ULTIMATE
TEACHER (SADGURU).
THE OUTER TEACHER IS MERELY A
MILESTONE. IT IS ONLY YOUR INNER
TEACHER THAT WILL WALK WITH
YOU TO THE GOAL,
FOR HE IS THE GOAL.

NISARGADATTA   MAHARAJ

SUMMARY

The **I AM**, which is made of **CONSCIOUSNESS**, if "stayed" with acts as a portal or gateway to the absolute. It seems that not always, but *generally* before this "occurs," the outer reflections of **CONSCIOUSNESS**, which appear to be separate from the **I AM**, are cut. Soon, the **I AM** is all there is. This pure **I AM** is the Guru. When you become the **I AM**, "it" leads "you" beyond, to the **CONSCIOUSNESS,** which the **I AM** is made of. Upon the **I AM**'s evaporation, the **CONSCIOUSNESS** and the **NOTHINGNESS** beyond, into the **NAMELESS ABSOLUTE**, "to" the **BIG SILENCE** is *realized*.

Question: Why is there no bhakti devotion in what you are saying?

I AM A BHAKTI, I AM AN ATMA BHAKTI, I WORSHIP MYSELF.

NISARGADATTA MAHARAJ

To truly understand this statement we must first understand that bhakti is devotion. True bhakti, or the fruit of bhakti, occurs when the devotee (or bhakta) and the object of devotion **Guru-I AM** are one. Since the **CONSCIOUSNESS** which condenses down to become the **I AM** is the source of all deities and is the **GURU**, to "abide in the **I AM** is the purest bhakti"; to discard all else, the purest road and form of devotion.

THE BEINGNESS ITSELF IS THE GURU.

(PG. 54, THE ULTIMATE MEDICINE)

THE GURU

Volumes have been written on Gurus, their "purpose," actions, lessons, disciples, grace, etc. But what is a guru? A guru is someone who both *apperceives* that everything is made of the same **CONSCIOUSNESS**, while simultaneously knowing that all of it, including the **GURU**, is a *mirage*. According to Nisargadatta Maharaj, the **I AM** is the inner teacher or guru. When your own **SELF**, the **I AM,** is realized the "pull" or need for the "outer" teacher or Guru vanishes. Furthermore, when the **I AM** is abided in, then the *apprehension* of the **BIG EMPTINESS** is realized.

THAT WHICH SEES ALL OF THIS AND THE NOTHING TOO IS THE INNER TEACHER. HE IS YOUR OWN SELF.

NISARGADATTA MAHARAJ

THE GURU AS TEACHER

For "me", most Gurus were not the powerful or strong *teachers* that "I" needed. It was Nisargadatta Maharaj's on-going fury, his *in-your-face* confrontation, which shocked and shattered the person which was a reflection of the **CONSCIOUSNESS** of **I AM**, which "I" did not know was false. At first, this was extremely painful, but ultimately it forcibly made me aware of the **I AM** and the **CONSCIOUSNESS** behind it.

"ANYONE COMING HERE WILL BE LIQUIDATED."

NISARGADATTA MAHARAJ

Nisargadatta Maharaj's words were so direct, powerful, succinct, and shocking, that oftentimes I would stay in bed for weeks at a time before I could go back and withstand the next blow to "myself" (my ego), and the concepts I thought were "me". "I" always knew his aim, and knew if I stayed the course, as he said to me, "**IT WILL BE REVEALED TO YOU.**"

WITH THOSE WORDS OF THE GURU, YOUR BODY-MIND HAD A SHOCK BECAUSE THE DISSOLUTION BEGAN

NISARGADATTA MAHARAJ
(Pg. 129, The Nectar Of Immortality)

THE OUTER GURU AS A PERSON

THEY (THE REALIZED) MAY LAUGH OR CRY ACCORDING TO CIRCUMSTANCES. BUT INWARDLY, THEY ARE COOL AND CLEAR, WATCHING DETACHEDLY THEIR OWN SPONTANEOUS REACTIONS. APPEARANCES ARE MISLEADING AND MORE SO IN THE CASE OF THE GNANI

NISARGADATTA MAHARAJ
(Pg. 529, I Am That)

This is a statement that both confounds and confuses people who are not established as **THAT** or aware of **THAT ONE SUBSTANCE**. Because from every other level the behavior of a Guru can appear crazy and even contradictory to what we imagine it should be. For the unrealized who lack vision and understanding, a guru, *should* always be perfect, appropriate, non-judgmental, never angry, always loving and compassionate, wise, chaste, etc., etc.. These are illusions. Because as the body-mind of the Guru continues its destiny as **CONSCIOUSNESS** called Guru, they (the Guru) know it is all a *mirage*, which has nothing to do with them.

THE INNER GURU IS NOT COMMITTED TO NON-VIOLENCE.HE CAN BE QUITE VIOLENT AT TIMES TO THE POINT OF DESTROYING THE OBTUSE OR PERVERTED PERSONALITY.

NISARGADATTA MAHARAJ
(Pg. 373, I Am That)

In the West, at this moment in time, the confrontation of the teacher is greatly misunderstood. The personality must be seen for what it is. This process can oftentimes be quite confrontative and painful. Maharaj was not a passive open-hearted little **Mahatma**. He was a confrontative force that smashed the self-deceit of the personality, so that the **I AM** would stabilize.

THE DIFFICULTY LIES NOT WITH THE GURU. IT IS THE RIPE DISCIPLE WHICH IS LACKING WHEN A PERSON IS NOT READY WHAT CAN BE DONE.

NISARGADATTA MAHARAJ
(Pg. 374, I Am That)

In this way, they are free. This does not mean doing what they want. It means they are free of the body-mind-lens, although, from the outside, they seem like everyone else.

Question: Many eastern teachings and teachers seem foreign and exotic and more exciting than Western teachers. Why?

Stephen: Because in our culture, we like what is different. If they are too much like us, people imagine that they cannot "possess" the *realization*. One must understand that there is no rigid standard of outward qualities for one who is realized. They just know who they are, and that you and they and everything are made of **CONSCIOUSNESS** and is a *mirage*.

GURU AND DISCIPLE

The model of an *outer* Guru can be an important beginning step. It *can be* significant at first to have someone who not only knows who they are or that **THEY ARE NOT** - but can also teach, pull, or show the **I AM** and beyond, until the outer is realized as the inner self **I AM** and then is no longer needed. Shortly after Nisargadatta met his Guru Sri Siddharameshwar Maharaj, he died. However, enough was given or understood so that the inner **SELF-I AM** was all that was needed. In reality the **I AM** is the true Guru or Sat Guru. The outer guru was merely a phenomenon, a guide. The "inner" or **I AM** and later **CONSCIOUSNESS** were the true Guru.

CALL THE KNOWLEDGE I AM THE GURU.

(Pg., 128, The Nectar of Immortality)

The worship, "focus" once the outer evaporates (which does take time), is ongoing as the **VOID-SELF** dissolves the "I"

or "self" consciousness, including awareness (awar*er*) even the
VOID beyond itself.

Question: I have heard from different Gurus that pure devo-
               tion is to be the dust of the Guru's feet. What is the
               dust of the guru's feet?

Stephen: The dust of the guru's feet is a metaphor written about
               for centuries, which does not clearly explain its true
               meaning and *apperception.* The Guru is **THAT
               VOID OF UNDIFFERENTIATED CON-
               SCIOUSNESS,** "you" as the dust of the **VOID,**
               "you" are like cosmic dust in the vastness of the **BIG
               EMPTINESS.** To be the dust of the Guru's feet
               means to realize that you are merely like the cosmic
               dust of the **VOID** or **THAT**. Imagine within the vast-
               ness is a piece of cosmic dust. In this metaphor the
               vastness of outer space is the Guru—the dust—you.
               And, as the dust dissolves into the vastness of outer
               space there is no you and no Guru.

Nine

THE VOID

. . . .

I AM NOTHING
I AM COMPLETELY VOID

NISARGADATTA MAHARAJ
(Pg. 59, Seeds Of Consciousness)

THE FINAL ANSWER IS THIS:
NOTHING IS.

NISARGADATTA MAHARAJ
(Pg. 415, I Am That)

THE VOID

The **VOID** or **PURE EMPTINESS** is or has also been called **CONSCIOUSNESS**, which really means **UNDIFFEREN-TIATED CONSCIOUSNESS** (no-subject object), or NO-I, the **VOID** or underlying unity, **GOD**, and the divine substance, etc.

Any word you use to describe it, *IS NOT IT*, nor does it adequately say what it is. Why? Because the underlying unity or Quantum Consciousness is not something out there but is here, there, everywhere. It is what everything is made of. Although there appears to be one or more substances, things, objects, events, per-ceivers, **GODS**, etc., in actuality, this is an illusion, a *mirage* – there is only **THAT ONE SUBSTANCE** and **YOU** and **I AM THAT**.

THE WORLD SPROUTS INTO BEING OUT
OF NOTHING AND RETURNS TO NOTHING.

NISARGADATTA MAHARAJ

There are few Nisargadatta statements which so clearly demonstrate that everything is **EMPTINESS**, and that form is con-densed **EMPTINESS**; or the Buddhist Heart Sutra, **EMPTINESS** is none other that form, form is none other than **EMPTINESS**.

Because the **VOID** is and becomes all we see, hear, do, or imagine, including the imagin*er* and the "I" that imagines, there is no place where it is not. It is also everything and, as everything, it is **ALL THAT IS**.

THE VOID BEYOND BEING AND NON BEING
BEYOND CONSCIOUSNESS,
THIS VOID IS ALSO FULLNESS.

NISARGADATTA MAHARAJ
(Pg. 392, I Am That)

It is that **VOID**, which is **UNDIFFERENTIATED CON-SCIOUSNESS,** which Buddha, or **GOD** is made of and from. We could say it is **VOID**, but it is everything so we could also call it fullness. In this way the **VOID**, is full or Empty or neither. When students asked him, "How long does it take to realize this?" he responded by saying,

"YOU WILL GET MATURITY QUICKLY IF YOU WOULD
STAY PUT IN YOUR NOTHINGNESS."

NISARGADATTA MAHARAJ

BEING WITH
NISARGADATTA MAHARAJ

Nisargadatta continually said to me, "**IT WILL BE RE-VEALED TO YOU.**" At the time I thought, how interesting, or *when,* but truly oftentimes "I" thought "I" forgot his words as "I" went through my life.

As years passed and layers naturally (**NISARGA**) shed, and Quantum Psychology was born and died, his words like a seed sprouted, and the *mirage* was seen as the *mirage.*

NOW WHAT YOU HAVE LEARNED HERE BECOMES THE SEED. YOU MAY FORGET IT - APPARENTLY. BUT IT WILL LIVE, AND, IN DUE SEASON, SPROUT AND GROW AND BRING FLOWERS AND FRUIT. ALL WILL HAPPEN BY ITSELF.

(Pg. 242, I AM THAT)

There was always a fear and yet an extraordinary desire to interact with Maharaj. I felt an irresistible urge to realize and discover, **WHO I WAS**, and so "I" was drawn into his words, and these words lead me into the bottomlessness of **NOTHINGNESS**.

EVERYTHING IS AFRAID OF NOTHING, FOR WHEN A THING TOUCHES NOTHING IT BECOMES NOTHING. IT IS LIKE A BOTTOMLESS PIT WHATEVER FALLS INTO IT DISAPPEARS.

NISARGADATTA MAHARAJ

(Pg. 88, I Am That)

I do not want to mislead people into thinking that self-concepts and ideas just met the **NOTHING** of Nisargadatta and disappeared or evaporated. These concepts had a life of their own, a fight-flight survival, which, as it and the "I" "I" "thought" "I" was knew, that its evaporation was inevitable. In this way it was oftentimes a painful death for the "I," "I" thought "I" was.

I AM THAT— COSMIC CONSCIOUSNESS

I once said to him; "I cannot stop coming here. What is this desire?" And he said, "You have won the grace of your true nature." "Does it matter in what form this grace comes?" I asked and he fired back, **"You think you are a person so you think Maharaj is a person, you think you are an entity or deity, so you think Maharaj is an entity or deity . Maharaj is not a person, an entity, or a deity. Maharaj is COSMIC CONSCIOUSNESS."**

BEYOND IT ALL THERE IS VOID.
THIS VOID IS ONE FOR ALL.

NISARGADATTA MAHARAJ
(Pg. 378, I Am That)

THE OBSERVER
AND THE OBSERVED

THE OBSERVER AND HIS OBSERVATION
AS WELL AS THE WORLD
OBSERVED APPEAR AND DISAPPEAR TOGETHER.

NISARGADATTA MAHARAJ

One of the crucial understandings of Nisargadatta is that there is not just one observer, but an infinite number. And that a new observer arises and subsides with each observed.

To realize the **I AM**, just notice a thought, observe the thought, and then ask yourself, "What observer is observing that?." Notice you go blank. That blank stateless state or No-State state is the non-verbal **I AM.** Stay with it and allow your awareness to move or expand backward and notice the **EMPTINESS** or **VOID.** This truly is a stateless state because, although there is a state, it is not describable - it is **NOTHING.**

YOU ARE THE CHANGELESS BACKGROUND, AGAINST WHICH CHANGES ARE PERCEIVED.

NISARGADATTA MAHARAJ

(PG. 353, I AM THAT)

If you could now, eyes closed, notice you are the background and thoughts the foreground. Notice the background always remains the same even as the foreground continually appears to change. Soon, the background, the experience*r*, and the experience are seen as the same substance as the foreground, and everything dissolves.

THE EXPERIENCER AND THE EXPERIENCE ARE BOTH TO BE DISSOLVED.

NISARGADATTA MAHARAJ

At some point, it becomes clear that all "spiritual" or identity work, or any work you have been doing on this alleged self, is not being done by a "you" Rather, "you" begin to "see" that the **EMPTINESS** is dissolving the illusion that the "I" is made of a different substance. It is like water droplets (I-dentities) evaporating in the sunlight. Soon there is an *apperception* that it is only an illusion that an "I" was doing anything.

Question: Then what's the point? Why do "spiritual" practice at all?

Stephen: There is no point. You keep separating the "I" from the **VOID OF UNDIFFERENTIATED CONSCIOUSNESS** - so you imagine you do. There is only the **VOID**.

And even this is not so. Because, it can only be seen, known, or experienced as long as there is an "awar*er* or know*er*" that has this knowledge. When the know*er* who has this knowledge is no more - then the "I" doing this or that, or the **VOID** being the doer of this or that also evaporates. When the "I" and **VOID** are realized as the same substance, the "I" is no more and there is no you.

The concepts an individual holds or has is part of the concept of an individual itself. In other words, the concept and the "I", which believes the concept, are one unit. To illustrate, if there is a concept called "I am bad" *the "I" is in the concept "I am Bad."* In this way, concepts are brought *on screen* and into awareness through confrontation and enquiry so that it can destroy the "I" that one thinks one is, which is who they are in the context of the *mirage*.

RENUNCIATION

ATTACHMENT IS BORN ALONG WITH THE SENSE OF "I" AND "MINE." FIND THE TRUE MEANING OF THESE WORDS AND YOU WILL BE FREE OF BONDAGE.

(Pg. 386, I Am That)

THE I-ME-MINE AND MY

Baba Muktananda wrote an essay called, *The Secret of Renunciation*. According to Muktananda, there was no need to renounce the world, one must only renounce the **I-ME-MINE**. In the same way, to remain in the No-State state of no thoughts memory, emotions, associations, perceptions, attention or intentions **CONSCIOUSNESS**'s reflecting through the **I AM** must be dismantled so that there is no longer any identification with I-me-mine and my. How does one begin to question and dismantle the **I-ME-MINE** and **MY**. Below is a short edited transcribed interaction with a student which might help to provide a clue or hint into this enquiry process.

ENQUIRING INTO THE NATURE OF "I":
AN OVERVIEW

Part I:

1. What idea does the concept of **I AM** have about the concept of *I*?
2. Why would the concept of **I AM** come up with that concept?
3. If that was just a concept of **I AM** and was made of the same **CONSCIOUSNESS** as **I AM** and had nothing to with anything, . . ?
4. (Repeat until nothing arises.)

ENQUIRY INTO THE NATURE OF "ME":
AN OVERVIEW

Part II:

1. What idea does the concept of the **I AM** have about the concept of *me*?
2. Why would the concept of **I AM** come up with that concept?
3. If that was just a concept of **I AM** and was made of the same **CONSCIOUSNESS** as **I AM** and had nothing to with anything, . . ?
4. (Repeat until nothing arises.)

ENQUIRY INTO THE NATURE OF "MINE":
AN OVERVIEW

Part III:

1. What idea does the concept of the **I AM** have about the concept of *mine*?
2. Why would the concept of **I AM** come up with that concept?
3. If that was just a concept of **I AM** and was made of the same **CONSCIOUSNESS** as **I AM** and had nothing to with anything, . . ?
4. (Repeat until nothing arises.)

ENQUIRY INTO THE NATURE OF MY:
AN OVERVIEW

Part IV:
1. What idea does the concept of the **I AM** have about the concept of *My*.
2. Why would the concept of **I AM** come up with that concept?
3. If that was just a concept of **I AM** and was made of the same **CONSCIOUSNESS** as **I AM** and had nothing to with anything, . . ?
4. (Repeat until nothing arises)

The reader is suggested to follow and allow the Enquiry to happen.

AN ENQUIRY DEMONSTRATION INTO THE NATURE OF THE "I"

Part I - The concept of "I"

Wolinsky: Where is the concept **I AM** that believes in the concept of "I"?

Student: My chest.

Wolinsky: What idea does the concept of **I AM** have about the concept of *"I"*?

Student: That the *"I"* is separate from it.

Wolinsky: Why would the concept of **I AM** come up with that concept?

Student: _____Silence_____Blank.

Wolinsky: If that was just a concept that belonged to the con-
                cept of **I AM** and was made of the same **CON-
                SCIOUSNESS** as **I AM** and had nothing to do with
                anything. . . ?

Student: _____Silence_____Blank.

Note:
**Oftentimes the enquiry leads one to go blank,
the blank is either said, or not said with silence
or there is a gesture of the hands implying, there
is nothing going on. This is an indicator of the
non-verbal I AM; (no thoughts, memory, emotions, associations, perceptions, attention or intentions), or the BIG EMPTINESS with no
words.**

Wolinsky: Any other ideas the concept of **I AM** has about the
                concept of *"I"*?

Student: That the *"I"* is its reflection.

Wolinsky: Why would the concept of **I AM** come up with that
                concept?

Student: _____Silence_____Blank.

Wolinsky: If that was just a concept of **I AM** and was made of
                the same **CONSCIOUSNESS** as **I AM** and had
                nothing to do with anything. . . ?

Student: _____Silence_____Blank.

Wolinsky: What other ideas does the concept of **I AM** have
                about the concept of "I"?

Student: That the *"I"* is made of the same substance as **I AM**

Wolinsky: Why would the concept of **I AM** come up with that
                concept?

Student: _____long silence.

AN ENQUIRY DEMONSTRATION
INTO THE NATURE OF
THE COMCEPT OF ME

Part II: The Concept of ME

Wolinsky: Where is the concept of **I AM** which believes in the concept of "me"?

Student: My throat.

Wolinsky: What idea could the concept of **I AM** have about the concept of ME?

Student: Me is me and the body is me

Wolinsky: Why would the concept of **I AM** come with that concept?

Student: It is just a way the **I AM** identifies itself as a thing like the body.

Wolinsky: If that was just a concept of the **I AM** and was made of the same **CONSCIOUSNESS** as **I AM** and had nothing to do with anything. . . ?

Student: _____Blank.

Wolinsky: What other idea could the concept of **I AM** have about the concept of ME?

Student: It is.

Wolinsky: Why would the concept of **I AM** come up with the concept of *IS*?

Student: Because it wants to be.

Wolinsky: If *BE* and *IS* were just concepts of the **I AM** and was
                made of the same **CONSCIOUSNESS** as **I AM** and
                had nothing to do with anything. . .?

Student: _____Long Silence.

Wolinsky: What other idea could the concept of **I AM** have
                about the concept of ME?

Student: That it has a location like here.

Wolinsky: Why would the concept of **I AM** come up with the
                concept of location?

Student: Because to locate is to *BE*.

Note:
**Here we will separate the *BE* concept from the
concept of location.**

Wolinsky: If the concept of *BE* is separate from the concept of
                location, then.

Student: _____Blank_____Silence.

Wolinsky: What other ideas does the concept of **I AM** have
                about the concept of ME?

Student: _____**NOTHING**_____Silence.

AN ENQUIRY DEMONSTRATION INTO THE NATURE OF THE CONCEPT OF MINE

Part III: The Concept of Mine.

Wolinsky: Where in the body is the concept of **I AM** which believes in the concept of "mine"?

Student: Right arm and hand.

Wolinsky: What idea could the concept of **I AM** have about the concept of Mine?

Student: *Mine* belongs to *"I."*

Wolinsky: What other idea the could concept of **I AM** have about the concept of Mine?

Student: That I-me-mine and **I AM** are all together.

NOTE:
Here we will separate all concepts from the I AM so that there is just pure I AM.

Wolinsky: If the "I" is separate from "me" which is separate from **I AM** then. . . ?

Student: There's no location.

Wolinsky: Why would the concept of **I AM** come up with a concept called location?

Student: _____Long Silence.

Wolinsky: What other ideas could concept of **I AM** have about the concept of *Mine*?

Student: That it is.

Wolinsky: Why would the concept of **I AM** come up with the concept of *IS*?

Student: The IS concept is part of the I-ME-Mine concept.

Wolinsky: What occurs if we were to separate *IS* from I-me-mine and they were all separate concepts?

Student: _____Long Silence.

Note:
What holds concepts together are their associations. When we separate the associations, the concepts lose their power and dissolve.

Wolinsky: If all this was just concepts of the **I AM** and were made of the same **CONSCIOUSNESS** as **I AM** and had nothing to do with anything. . . ?

Student: _____Blank_____Long Silence.

Note:
CONSCIOUSNESS "condenses" to become the I AM and reflects out the I, me, mine, my which are all reflections of CONSCIOUSNESS, made of CONSCIOUSNESS, and never lose their true nature as CONSCIOUSNESS.

Wolinsky: What other ideas does the concept of **I AM** have about the concept of mine?

Student: Something to do with possession.

Wolinsky: Why would the concept of **I AM** come up with the concept of possessions?

Student: _____Long Silence.

Wolinsky: If possession was just a concept of the **I AM** and
            was made of the same **CONSCIOUSNESS** as **I AM**
            and had nothing to do with anything. . .?

Student: _____Silence.

AN ENQUIRY DEMONSTRATION INTO THE
NATURE OF THE CONCEPT OF MY
Part IV: The Concept of MY

Wolinsky: Where is the concept of **I AM** which believes in the
            concept of "MY"?

Student: Torso.

Wolinsky: What idea could the concept of **I AM** have about the
            concept of *MY*?

Student: *My* reflects and belongs to mine.

Wolinsky: Why would the concept of **I AM** come up with that
            concept?

Student: To give the Mine ownership and location.

Wolinsky: If ownership and location were just concepts of the
            I AM and was made of the same **CONSCIOUS-
            NESS** as **I AM** and had nothing to do with any-
            thing...?

Student: _____Silence.

Wolinsky: What other ideas could the concept of **I AM** have
            about the concept of *my*?

Student: It is body related.

Wolinsky: Why would the concept of **I AM** come up with the concept of something being body related?

Student: It helps in the body's survival.

Wolinsky: If the survival was just a concept of the **I AM** and was made of the same **CONSCIOUSNESS** as **I AM** and had nothing to do with anything. . ?

Student: _____Silence.

Wolinsky: If **I AM** has nothing to do with I-Me-Mine-My survival, then. . . ?

Student: _____Long Silence.

Note:

Here we are separating the I AM from the reflections of CONSCIOUSNESS, thus leaving us intermittently with the blank, the No-State state of I AM and ultimately with pure CONSCIOUSNESS.

Wolinsky: If all of this were just a concept of the **I AM** and was made of the same **CONSCIOUSNESS** as **I AM** and had nothing to do with anything. . .?

Student: _____Long Silence.

Wolinsky: What other ideas could the concept of **I AM** have about the concept of MY?

Student: None.

Wolinsky: If the concept of I-me-mine-my all were reflections of **CONSCIOUSNESS** through the **I AM** then. . . ?

Student: _____Blank_____**NOTHINGNESS.**

Wolinsky: If the concept of **I AM** and the concept of I, me,
              mine and my were all made of the same **CON-
              SCIOUSNESS** then. . . ?

Student: Everything is gone - it disappears

Wolinsky: If the concept of **I AM** and I-me-mine-my were all a
              mirage, which was made of the same **CONSCIOUS-
              NESS**, and had nothing to do with anything then?

Student: _____Long Long Silence.

CONFRONTATION

Question: Why is there so much emphasis on confrontation; it
              seems so violent?

Stephen: The purpose of confrontation is to bring into aware-
              ness (*"on-screen"*) concepts about oneself which
              were, or are, not in awareness (*on-screen*). It is only
              the "I" an I-dentity that is being confronted, it is the
              "I" you think you are. It is only concepts. *It* (the "I"
              or "Identity") feels the pain and violence because
              the I-dentity goes into survival and because you think
              you are your ideas and I-dentities. The purpose of
              confrontation is to bring *on-screen* and into aware-
              ness the unquestioned concepts that you have not
              even realized are concepts so that they can be ques-
              tioned and gone beyond.

YOU CANNOT LET GO OF
SOMETHING UNTIL YOU KNOW
WHAT IT IS

NISARGADATTA MAHARAJ

THE NON-DOER

Question: If there is no **VOID** doing then who or what is the
              doer?

Stephen: It is better to understand that *THERE IS NO DOER*,
              rather than *I am not the doer*. I am not the doer im-
              plies there is a doer (like GOD or VOID) and doing.
              THERE IS NO DOER because all doer-doing-done
              appears in the context of the *mirage* only - There is
              no doer-doing-done. The concept of a **VOID** eating
              a concept of a you or a **VOID** as the doer can only
              exist if there is a know*er* with that knowledge to say
              it is so.

     Therefore, anything dependent upon an awar*er* and know*er*
will always be dependent upon a know*er*-awar*er* being there. This
involves five concepts, 1) an awar*er* or know*er*; 2) the **VOID**; 3)
awareness; 4) knowledge or consciousness of something; and 5) a
you.
     All of these are dependent upon the concept **I AM** and all
the **I AM**'s knowledge occurs in the context of the *mirage*. All are
concepts and eventually even the **I AM** with all its concepts and
knowledge will also dissolve and be no longer.

"SEE IT ALL AS A DREAM AND HAVE DONE WITH IT"

NISARGADATTA MAHARAJ

Question: But you do teach about the **VOID**?

Answer: The **VOID** is the screen that **CONSCIOUSNESS**
              appears on. You cannot have one without the other
              there is no separate **VOID**. There is only a **VOID** of
              UNDIFFERENTIATED CONSCIOUSNESS, and

hence no VOID. There is only a **VOID** if there is **CONSCIOUSNESS** there to say it is so.

ENQUIRY INTO THE NATURE OF THE KNOWER

Enquiry Step I:	Notice a thought.
Enquiry Step II:	Notice the knower of the thought.
Enquiry Step III:	Notice that you go blank when "I" say, "What knower is knowing that?" Or
Enquiry Step III:	*Variation*: *Apperceive* the knower and the thought as the same substance.

The knower of the thought is part of the thought itself. That is why you go blank. *There is no separate self which is having a separate experience.* The concept of a self is part of the thought itself. The concept of self is contained within the experience of a self. Once you realize the self is only a concept that arises with each new "experience," then you "get" that there is no self.

Question: What about **I AM THAT**, isn't that enlightenment?

Stephen: I once asked Maharaj about *So-Ham*, *Ham-Sa* mantra. So-Ham, Ham-Sa means **I AM THAT–THAT I AM**. He said to me, "**If I write on a piece of paper 1,000 pounds of gold is that the same as 1,000 pounds of gold?**" You must mediate past your concepts. One of the most frequent questions is; what does Nisargadatta Maharaj mean by **I AM THAT** or enlightenment? It can best be described again in his own words:

THE WORD THAT
IN THE STATEMENT REFERS TO EVERYTHING
THAT IS IN THE TOTALITY.

NISARGADATTA MAHARAJ
(PG. 24, THE NECTAR OF IMMORTALITY)

You can never say what enlightenment is - only what enlightenment isn't. The idea or description of the thing is not the thing, because it requires a separate descriptor. The concept of spirituality and enlightenment are only an appearance in **CONSCIOUSNESS**. The **I AM** is the glue which holds this "experience" of the *mirage* together. No **I AM**, no *mirage*. So **I AM THAT** - is not **I AM THAT**.

YOUR TRUE HOME
IS IN NOTHINGNESS:
IN EMPTINESS ALL IS CONTENT.

NISARGADATTA MAHARAJ
(Pg. 487, I Am That)

Ten

THE BIRTH AND DEATH CONCEPTS

. . . .

TAKE THE IDEA, "I WAS BORN."
YOU MAY TAKE IT TO BE TRUE.
IT IS NOT. YOU WERE NEVER BORN
NOR WILL YOU EVER DIE. IT IS THE
IDEA WHICH WAS BORN AND SHALL
DIE. NOT YOU.

NISARGADATTA MAHARAJ
(Pg. 392, I Am That)

BIRTH AND DEATH
CONCEPTION: TO BRING FORTH CONCEPTS

ENQUIRE INTO THE BIRTH PRINCIPLE

NISARGADATTA MAHARAJ
(pg. 45, Consciousness and the Absolute)

The concept of birth and death lies at the very root of who we think we are. Most so-called "spiritual" systems' talk of birth and what will happen when - or if - one dies. From being born for karmic reasons to missions, from the illusion of purposes to lessons, we are all bombarded with the resistance to the concept of death. When I was with Maharaj, a student asked, "What's the purpose?"

THERE IS NO PURPOSE

NISARGADATTA MAHARAJ

ALL OF THESE CONCEPTS ONLY SUPPORT, AND ARE FOUNDED ON, THE FALSE CONCEPT I AM, AND BOLSTER AND RE-ENFORCE THE EGO OR "I".

PRIOR TO YOUR BIRTH, YOU HAD NO KNOWLEDGE "YOU WERE" AND THAT YOU EXPERIENCED MILLIONS OF BIRTHS. CAN SUCH A STORY BE BELIEVED AT ALL?

NISARGADATTA MAHARAJ
(Pg. 73, The Nectar Of Immortality)

However, the purpose of enquiry and confrontation is to bring us into the light of awareness *ALL* concepts so that they can be seen as false and discarded. For sure, birth and death, when they remain unquestioned, have power and depth. Death cannot be an issue unless one believes in birth. Birth cannot be an issue if one does not know **I AM.**

REINCARNATION

Nisargadatta Maharaj was not into reincarnation or rebirth and karma:

ALL STORIES OF REINCARNATION AND REBIRTH ARE MERE STORIES MEANT FOR THE IGNORANT MASSES.

NISARGADATTA MAHARAJ

Upon hearing this "I" was reminded of the Yoga Vasistha, one of India's greatest spiritual texts. Vasistha was Prince Ram's guru (before Prince Ram knew he was Lord Ram). Vasistha teaches Prince Ram about Kundalini Yoga, and chakras. After explaining all of this, Vasistha asks Ram to tell him what he understood. Ram replies with the chakra story which he had just been told. Vasistha tells him, *this is not* it. When Ram asked, "Why did you teach me this then?" Vasistha replies, "These stories are just for the *unen-*lightened," and that none of this exists. Vasistha then says, "Every-thing is **CONSCIOUSNESS**; nothing exists outside of **CONSCIOUSNESS**".

THE BIRTH CONCEPT

THERE IS NO OTHER CONCEPT EXCEPT THAT "I AM BORN" AND THAT IS THE PRIMORDIAL ILLUSION.

NISARGADATTA MAHARAJ
(Pg. 103, Seeds Of Consciousness)

One of the most amazing *apperceptions* is that there is no birth or death and that these are unquestioned assumptions made of **CONSCIOUSNESS**. Imagine water in a *mirage* thinking, I must have come from somewhere - then imagining a *past or birth*, then developing explanations as to why it is there, its purpose, why it is warm water when it should be cold water, worrying about surviving or being overtaken by drought or rain, or what will happen when it dies. Now, if you were the water in the *mirage* that did not know you were a *mirage* - then you would not realize *you just appeared*, and that you had no inherent self-existence or self-nature.

Waking-up to your mirageness is the realization.

GOING BEYOND THE BIRTH — DEATH CONCEPTS:

Nisargadatta Maharaj said to "me":

THERE IS NO BIRTH.
THERE IS NO DEATH.
THERE IS NO PERSON.
IT IS ALL A CONCEPT.
IT'S ALL AN ILLUSION.

It took twelve years to "get" the profound realization that there was no birth or death, that they were only concepts within the context of a *mirage*.

Below is an example of an *enquiry* with a student around the birth-death concept. This enquiry can serve as a *hint* as to how to explore the birth-death concept. Please feel free to follow along with the enquiry and notice what, if anything, occurs.

ENQUIRY INTO THE NATURE OF THE CONCEPT OF DEATH

Wolinsky: Where in the body is the concept of the **I AM** which believes in the concept of death?

Student: Head and heart.

Wolinsky: How does the concept of **I AM** define death?

Student: The end of everything.

Wolinsky: What assumptions has the concept of **I AM** made about this concept of the end of everything?

Student: That it will be over.

Wolinsky: What have been the consequences for the **I AM** around this?

Student: To keep moving and doing to avoid this inevitability.

Wolinsky: Where now in this body is this concept of **I AM** which believes in this death concept?

Student: Still in my heart.

Note:
**The heart is a common place that the I AM sits.
Birth-death can be attached to the heart along
with manifest-unmanifest. This is why the heart
is referred to so frequently in spiritual work.
For example, the *heart* sutra, meditation on the
heart, or meditations on the *heart* of an enlightened being. In this sense, opening one's *heart* is
not about compassion, love, etc. - it is about
opening up to the infinite. Simply put your
physical heart is a metaphor. *Your real heart is
the Emptiness.***

Wolinsky: Regarding this concept of **I AM** which believes in
            the concept of death, how has this concept of **I AM**
            (imagined it) deceived another concept of **I AM**?

Student: By playing the game as if death were real.

Wolinsky: And if this were part of the concept of **I AM** and had
            nothing to do with anything. . . ?

Student: _____Blank_____Silence.

Wolinsky: How has the concept of **I AM** deceived itself around
            the concept of death?

Student: That death was, that there was an end.

Wolinsky: And if that was only a concept of the **I AM** and had
            nothing to do with anything. . . ?

Student: _____Silence.

Wolinsky: Does this concept of death which belongs to the con-
            cept of **I AM** have any frozen feelings...?

Student: Grief.

Wolinsky: If the grief concept were only part of the concept of
             I AM and had nothing do with anything. . . ?

Student: _____Silence.

Wolinsky: Does this concept of death, which belongs to the
             concept of **I AM**, have any frozen impulses?

Student: To survive.

Wolinsky: If this concept of survival belonged to the concept
             of **I AM** had nothing to do with anything. . . ?

Student: _____I'm gone_____Long Silence.

Wolinsky: Is there anything that this concept of **I AM** must not
             know about the concept of death?

Student: That there is not an *IS* or an *ISn't*.

Wolinsky: If the concept of IS or ISN'T were just concepts
             which were made of the same consciousness as **I
             AM** then_____?

Student: _____Long Silence.

Wolinsky: Is there anything else that this concept of **I AM** must
             not know about the concept of death?

Student: That there is no knowing

Wolinsky: If this concept of knowing belonged to the concept
             of **I AM** and was made of the same **CONSCIOUS-
             NESS** as **I AM** and had nothing to do with any-
             thing...?

Student: _____Long Silence.

Wolinsky: Is there anything else that this concept of **I AM** must
             not know about the concept of death?

Student: _____No_____Silence.

Wolinsky: *Prior* to this concept of death, was there a thing called **CONSCIOUSNESS**?

Student :   No_____Silence.

Wolinsky: This concept of **CONSCIOUSNESS,** which be-lieves in the concept of **I AM** and the death con-cept—if this concept of **CONSCIOUSNESS** was what the *mirage* and the **I AM** and the concept of death were all made of and it had nothing to do with anything...?

Student: Blank_____Silence.

Wolinsky: What lie could the concept of **CONSCIOUSNESS** tell the concept of **I AM**?

Student: It is - was - will be and it has a beginning middle and end.

Wolinsky: And if these were just concepts of **CONSCIOUS-NESS** and had nothing to do with anything. . . ?

Student: _____Silence.

Wolinsky: Is there anything that this concept of **I AM**, with its concept of death, must not know?

Student: That the idea of *IS* or *ISN'T* is a concept born of **CONSCIOUSNESS** that isn't or rather blank_____**NOTHINGNESS.**

TO GROUP: The **I AM** is the primal concept of **CONSCIOUS-NESS**. The concept of death is a concept of the con-cept of **I AM** and is a concept made of **CON-SCIOUSNESS** and is true only in the context of the *mirage* - if that was not true - notice what occurs now.

ENQUIRY INTO THE NATURE
OF THE CONCEPT OF BIRTH

Wolinsky: Where in the body is the concept of **I AM** which believes in the concept of birth.

Student: My heart.

Note:
Again notice the heart I AM relationship.

Wolinsky: Ask the **I AM** to define birth.

Student: A beginning.

Wolinsky: What assumptions has the concept of **I AM** made about this concept of a beginning birth?

Student: That it occurred.

Wolinsky: If that were just a concept of the concept of **I AM** and it all was made of the same **CONSCIOUSNESS** and had nothing to do with anything...?

Student: _____Silence.

Wolinsky: What has been the consequences for the **I AM** concept believing in the concept of a birth/beginning.

Student: That it *is* and that there was a time when it wasn't.

TIME IS A CHILD OF A BARREN WOMAN

NISARGADATTA MAHARAJ
(Pg. 30, The Nectar Of Immortality)

Wolinsky: How has the concept of **I AM** lied to itself around the concepts of a beginning and a birth?

Student: That it wasn't - then it was.

Wolinsky: Is there anything that this concept of **I AM** who believes in the concept of birth must not know?

Student: _____Blank.

Wolinsky: Any frozen concepts that the concept of **I AM** has about the concept of birth?

Student: To *be*.

Wolinsky: If this concept to **BE** or **BEING** were just concepts of the concept of **I AM**, all of which were made of the same **CONSCIOUSNESS** as **I AM** and had nothing to do with anything. . . ?

Student: Blank_____. Then it isn't or wasn't.

Wolinsky: If this *is* or *wasn't* was just a concept of the concept of **I AM** and was made of the same **CONSCIOUSNESS** as the **I AM** and had nothing to do with anything then. . . ?

Student: Blank_____.

Wolinsky: If all of this were just a concept of the concept of **I AM** and had nothing to do with anything. . . ?

Student: Blank_____ Long silence

Wolinsky: If this **CONSCIOUSNESS** which believes in the **I AM** beginning birth thing—if it too were just a concept that was made of the same substance as the **I AM** concept and birth concept and had nothing to do with anything. . . ?

Student: Blank_____Long silence.

Again;

THERE IS NO BIRTH.
THERE IS NO DEATH.
THERE IS NO PERSON.
IT'S ALL A CONCEPT.
IT'S ALL AN ILLUSION.

NISARGADATTA MAHARAJ

Eleven

ON CAUSE AND EFFECT

· ·

FOR ANYTHING, TO HAPPEN THE
ENTIRE UNIVERSE MUST COINCIDE. IT
IS WRONG TO BELIEVE THAT
ANYTHING, IN PARTICULAR CAN
CAUSE AN EVENT. EVERY CAUSE IS
UNIVERSAL. YOUR VERY BODY
WOULD NOT EXIST WITHOUT THE
ENTIRE UNIVERSE CONTRIBUTING TO
ITS CREATION AND SURVIVAL.

NISARGADATTA MAHARAJ
(Pg. 388, I Am That)

ON CAUSE AND EFFECT

NO THING IN EXISTENCE HAS A PARTICULAR CAUSE.

NISARGADATTA MAHARAJ

One of the greatest illusions is that of cause and effect. Although the concept of a specific (local) cause bringing out or causing a specific (local) effect was proved scientifically by John Stuart Bell in 1964 to *not be true* - still the human nervous system, being unable to "see" the ALL or totality of **THAT**, organizes cause-effect relationships where they do not exist.

ALL THAT HAPPENS IS THE CAUSE OF ALL THAT HAPPENS. CAUSES ARE NUMBERLESS, THE IDEA OF A SOLE CAUSE IS AN ILLUSION.

NISARGADATTA MAHARAJ

(PG. 398, I AM THAT)

This tendency of the nervous system to automatically assign one specific (local cause) and create a system which organizes chaos, provides the illusion of control. Furthermore, it provides reasons as to why things do or do not occur. This delusion makes us believe in this **FALSE CAUSE.** Further, it makes us believe that if we could just control what we believe to be the (**FALSE**) cause, we could alter the present or future time outcomes (effect). This delusional tendency stands at the forefront not only of modern psychology but also "spirituality."

THERE CAN BE NO CASUAL CONNECTION BETWEEN PRACTICE AND WISDOM. BUT THE OBSTACLES TO WISDOM ARE DEEPLY AFFECTED BY PRACTICE.

NISARGADATTA MAHARAJ

(Pg. 379, I Am That)

This is probably one of the great paradoxes for many of the *new* **ADVAITA** teachers. There is a presupposition that doing a "spiritual" practice of some sort re-enforces the non-existent "I" since there is no-I and no-doer.

To handle this paradox is quite simple, understand that there is only **ONE SUBSTANCE** and that all that is or is not supposed to happen will happen or it won't. Applying this to "spiritual" practice means, you will only do it if you do; you won't if you don't. There is only **ONE SUBSTANCE** - no free will or volition - nor are there two or more separate substances.

Nisargadatta Maharaj responded to this paradox when asked about spiritual practice.

DO IT IF YOU ARE DOING IT— DON'T DO IT IF YOU ARE NOT DOING IT. THERE IS NOTHING YOU CAN DO TO SPEED IT (THE REALIZATION) UP OR SLOW IT (THE REALIZATION) DOWN

NISARGADATTA MAHARAJ

Looking at Nisargadatta Maharaj in the "light" of physics is not as difficult as one might imagine. Certainly pivotal concepts, which form our vision of the universe, are abstractions of the nervous system, and yet they have important resemblances to what Maharaj is saying. Let us begin by looking at some basic scientific premises which comprise Quantum Physics and see how they might relate to Nisargadatta Maharaj.

"There are no local causes or locations."

John Stuart Bell

This pivotal piece supercedes the now disproved theory of karma, but more important it demonstrates the failure of psycho-spiritual systems, and answers the questions; *Why doesn't X* (effect) (liberation) occur when *Y* (cause) "spiritual" practice is applied.

To illustrate this, imagine everything perceivable and conceivable is the water contained within a huge bathtub. In order for something to happen, every particle of water must "agree" that this is to happen and move in a way to support that movement.

This is also true of local (separate-individual) causes. Without the entire water going along with what is occurring, it cannot occur. In this way there are no separate individual causes or effects.

What about location, why no location? Because there is only water, even the perceiver of the water is part of the water. This means that since all location is only relative to position, and with only water there is no position and there is hence no location there is only **ONE SUBSTANCE (ADVAITA)**.

Prior to all of the physics dimensions forces and phenomena of energy, space, mass, time, distance location, electromagnetics, gravity, light, sound, earth (radiation weak), sun (radiation strong)—there was **NOTHING** which "appears to become" everything. "You," prior to these dimensions, are "understandable" in this context. But then the ever illusive illusion of how to "get" there when there is no there?

LOCATION

One of the difficult things to *apperceive* or *apprehend* is **NON-LOCALITY**. Especially when coupled with **I AM**, and **YOU ARE** in or exist in a particular location. To remedy this and use the context of **NISARGA YOGA**, below is a demonstration of an **ENQUIRY** with a student.

ENQUIRY INTO THE
NATURE OF LOCATION

Wolinsky: Where in the body is the concept of **I AM** which believes in the concept of location?

Student: All over.

Wolinsky: Ask the **I AM** to define location.

Student: It is here.

Wolinsky: Ask of the concept of **I AM** to describe it?

Student: It is like a space that is located here.

Wolinsky: What assumptions has the concept of **I AM** that believes in the concept of space, the concept of here, and the concept of location made?

Student: That it is here, all is in this space.

Note:
All concepts can contain a certain force or energy. Undifferentiated concepts have *more* force because we are combining concepts, hence they become more believable and more unquestioned and more difficult to give-up. For this reason, our first step in the enquiry is to differentiate and un-fuse the undifferentiated or fused concepts.

Wolinsky: If we separate the concept of here from the concept
             of space - what occurs?

Student: _____(No Words).

Wolinsky: If we separate the concept of here from the concept
             of space, what does not occur?

Student: _____Solidness, like here—all and even now.
             _____Silence.

Wolinsky: *If* we separate the concept of here from the concept
             of space, what, if anything gets resisted?

Student: Blank_____Silence.

Wolinsky: *If* we separate the concept of *here* from the concept
             space and from the concept of *time*, what_____?

Student: Blank_____Silence.

Wolinsky: By the **I AM** having this time-space-now concept,
             what have been the consequences?

Student: I am, here, now.

Wolinsky: *If* all of these including the **I Am** were just concepts
             made of the same **CONSCIOUSNESS** and had
             nothing to do with anything, then...?

Student: _____Blank_____Silence.

Wolinsky: *If* the **I AM** is separate from here-now-space-now...?

Student: **I AM**—but not in space-time location.

Wolinsky: And_____?

Student: **I AM**.

| Wolinsky: | Prior to **I AM**? |
| Student: | _____Silence. There is only **I AM** _____**NOTHINGNESS**. |

Wolinsky: And how does **I AM** seem to **I AM** now?

Student: It is.

Wolinsky: Stay there. And if the **I AM** and everything else were all of that same **CONSCIOUSNESS** and had nothing to do with anything, then . . . ?

Student: _____Long silence.

If you stay with **I AM**, let go of all else "it" acts like a gateway to the **CONSCIOUSNESS** which the **I AM** is made of and into the **NOTHINGESS**.

EVEN SPACE AND TIME ARE IMAGINED.

NISARGADATTA MAHARAJ

All of the physics dimensions make sense. However, all of the physics dimensions require a perceive*r* of them. The physics dimensions and forces are all contained within the *mirage* and are hence imagined as **CONSCIOUSNESS** plays the part of the perceive*r* (scientist) and the perceive*d* (physics dimensions). Simply put, all of the physics dimensions are perceivables made by a perceive*r* and part of the *mirage*.

ENQUIRY INTO THE NATURE
OF THE PHYSICS DIMENSIONS

Wolinsky: How does the concept of *Energy* seem to the con-
              cept of **I AM**?

Student: Like a swirling moving mass.

Wolinsky: If that was just a concept that belonged to the con-
              cept of **I AM** and the concept of **I AM** and the en-
              ergy concept were both made of the same **CON-
              SCIOUSNESS** which had nothing to do with any-
              thing, then...?

Student: Blank_____.

Wolinsky: How does the concept of *Space* seem to the concept
              of **I AM**?

Student: Like a dense emptiness, but with boundaries around
              it.

Wolinsky: *If* that was just a concept that belonged to the con-
              cept of **I AM** and the concept of **I AM** and the con-
              cept of space were both concepts made of the same
              CONSCIOUSNESS which had nothing to do with
              anything, then...?

Student: Quiet

TIME IS THE CHILD OF A BARREN WOMAN

(Pg. 30, The Nectar Of Immortality)

Wolinsky: How does *Time* seem to the concept of **I AM**?

Student: Like a linear line or Function Floating in space.

Wolinsky: *If* that was just a concept that belonged to the con-
                cept of **I AM** and the concept of **I AM** and the con-
                cept of time were both concepts which were made
                of the same **CONSCIOUSNESS** and had nothing
                to do with anything, then...?

Student: Blank_____Silence.

THE IDEA OF BEGINNING AND TIME
ARE IN CONSCIOUSNESS

NISARGADATTA MAHARAJ

Note:
**It is CONSCIOUSNESS which conceals itself,
and CONSCIOUSNESS which reveals itself
and its nature as a *mirage*. Even the concept of
time and space are made of CONSCIOUS-
NESS, which is the substance the *mirage* is made
of.**

Wolinsky: How does the concept of *Mass* seem to the concept
                of **I AM**?

Student: Like solidified energy with no movement.

Wolinsky: If that was just a concept that belonged to the con-
                cept of **I AM** and the concept of **I AM** and the con-
                cept of mass were both concepts which were made
                of the same **CONSCIOUSNESS** which had noth-
                ing to do with anything, then . . . ?

Student: Blank space, with a boundary around it.

AWARENESS AND MATTER
ARE THE ACTIVE AND PASSIVE
ASPECTS OF PURE BEING.

NISARGADATTA MAHARAJ
(Pg. 483, I Am That)

Wolinsky: How does the concept of *Distance* seem to the concept of **I AM**?

Student: Like two points separated by space and in time.

Wolinsky: *If* that was just a concept that belonged to the concept of the **I AM** and the concept of **I AM** and the concept of distances were both concepts which were made of the same **CONSCIOUSNESS** which had nothing to do with anything, then. . . ?

Student: Blank_____Silence.

Wolinsky: How does the concept of *Location* seem to the concept of **I AM**?

Student: Like a fixed point in space.

Wolinsky: *If* that was just a concept that belonged to the concept of the **I AM** and the concept of **I AM** and the concept of location were both concepts which were made of the same **CONSCIOUSNESS** which had nothing to do with anything, then . . . ?

Student: Dispersed, empty, still.

Wolinsky: How does the concept of *Cause-Effect* seem to the concept of **I AM**?

Student: Like a must, an assumption in linear space time.

Wolinsky: *If* that was just a concept that belonged to the con-
               cept of the **I AM** and the concept of **I AM** and the
               concept of cause-effect were both concepts which
               were made of the same **CONSCIOUSNESS** which
               had nothing to do with anything, then . . . ?

Student: Blank_____Silence.

Wolinsky: How does the concept of *Electro-magnetics* seem to
               the concept of **I AM**?

Student: Like a sparkling tube with electrical charge.

Wolinsky: *If* that was just a concept that belonged to the con-
               cept of the **I AM** and the concept of **I AM** and the
               concept of electromagnetics were both concepts
               which were made of the same **CONSCIOUSNESS**
               which had nothing to do with anything, then . . . ?

Student: _____**NOTHINGNESS.**

Wolinsky: How does the concept of the *Sun (strong force)* seem
               to the concept of **I AM**?

Student: Like the sun fixed in space giving off sunbursts.

Wolinsky: *If* that was just a concept that belonged to the con-
               cept of the **I AM** and the concept of **I AM** and the
               concept of a strong force (sun) were both concepts
               which were made of the same **CONSCIOUSNESS**
               which had nothing to do with anything, then...?

Student: _____**NOTHINGNESS.**

Wolinsky: How does the concept of *Earth (weak force)* seem
               to the concept of **I AM**?

Student: Like a disintegrating dissolving force which dissolves everything.

Wolinsky: *If* that was just a concept that belonged to the concept of the **I AM** and the concept of **I AM** and the concept of a weak force were both concept which were made of the same **CONSCIOUSNESS** which had nothing to do with anything, then...?

Student: There is not desolation, even desolation or creation is a *mirage*.

Wolinsky: How does the concept of *Sound* seem to the concept of **I AM**?

Student: Like a force traveling between two points in space—time floating in **EMPTINESS**.

Wolinsky: *If* that was just a concept that belonged to the concept of the **I AM** and the concept of **I AM** and the concept of sound were both concepts which were made of the same **CONSCIOUSNESS** which had nothing to do with anything, then . . . ?

Student: _____Blank_____It's all an illusion.

Wolinsky: How does the concept of *Light* seem to the concept of **I AM**?

Student: Like emptiness condensing, forming light.

Wolinsky: *If* that was just a concept that belonged to the concept of the **I AM** and the concept of **I AM** and the concept of light were both concepts which were made of the same **CONSCIOUSNESS** which had nothing to do with anything, then . . . ?

Student: There is no light or darkness, it's all an illusion.

Wolinsky: How does the concept of *Gravity* seem to the concept of **I AM**?

Student: Like a gluey force that holds things together. But a
                concept formed by condensed space.

Wolinsky: *If* that was just a concept that belonged to the concept of the **I AM** and the concepts of **I AM** and the
                concept of gravity were both concepts which were
                made of the same **CONSCIOUSNESS** which had
                nothing to do with anything, then...?

Student: Blank_____Silence. It's all a concept.

Wolinsky: How does the concept of the *Past* seem to the concept of **I AM**?

Student: Like an idea coming out of **EMPTINESS**.

Wolinsky: *If* that was just a concept that belonged to the concept of the **I AM** and the concept of **I AM** and the
                concept of a past were both concepts which were
                made of the same **CONSCIOUSNESS** which had
                nothing to do with anything, then...?

Student: _____**NOTHING**.

Wolinsky: How does the concept of the *Present* seem to the
                concept of **I AM**?

Student: Like an idea, it's like the **I AM** is looking into blank
                space and making up concepts. Like the space **I AM**
                is looking into is an easel that the **I AM** paints on.

Wolinsky: *If* that was just a concept that belonged to the concept of the **I AM** and the concept of **I AM** and the
                concept of present were both concepts which were
                made of the same **CONSCIOUSNESS** which had
                nothing to do with anything, then...?

Student: **NOTHINGNESS**.

Wolinsky: How does the concept of the *Body Person* seem to
                the concept of **I AM**?

Student: Like an etheric mass appearing on **EMPTINESS**,
                with a voice coming out of it which the **I AM** iden-
                tifies as it. There seems to be **I AM's** I-dentification
                with voice or sound.

Wolinsky: *If* we separate voice-sound from **I AM** and space
                then…?

Student: Absolutely still. **NOTHINGNESS**.

Wolinsky: *If* that was just a concept that belonged to the con-
                cept of the **I AM** and the concept of **I AM** and the
                concept of body-person were both concepts which
                were made of the same **CONSCIOUSNESS** which
                had nothing to do with anything, then…?

Student: _____Long silence. Like an idea or ma-
                terial substance that the **I AM** is part of and makes
                the world with.

Wolinsky: How does the concept of **CONSCIOUSNESS** seem
                to the concept of **I AM**?

Student: _____Long silence.

Wolinsky: *If* that was just a concept that belonged to the con-
                cept of the **I AM** and the concept of **I AM** and all
                concepts were made of the same **CONSCIOUS-
                NESS** which had nothing to do with anything,
                then…?

Student: _____long silence. **VOID**.

CLOSING STATEMENT

With the *apperception* beyond cause and effect, and the physics dimensions, most notably energy, space, mass, time, and location, just to name a few, "you" come to the **NOTHINGNESS** intermittently *"prior"* to the mirage, and like cosmic dust, a bubble universe made of **CONSCIOUSNESS** occurs which is made of the same substance as the mirage.

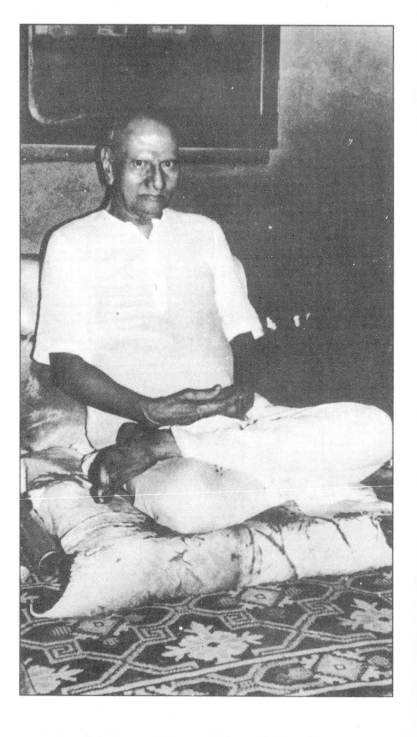

Twelve

THE MIRAGE

. . . .

WHATEVER CONCEPTS YOU HAVE
COLLECTED IN THIS WORLD ARE TOTALLY
USELESS. UNDERSTAND THAT THE TOTAL
MANIFESTATION IS THE CHILD OF
A BARREN WOMAN.

NISARGADATTA MAHARAJ

(PG. 43, Consciousness and The Absolute)

Mirage: **An optical illusion by which reflected objects are seen as real**

The notion of everything as an illusion or a dream is certainly not new.

However, the word *mirage* somehow seems to cut through its deeper meaning. When you use the word *illusion*, many imagine, "Yes it's all an illusion," or even, "Yes it's all a dream." But both subtly imply that there is a dream*er* or one who is not part of the illusion *who is*. The fact remains that not only is it all a *mirage*, but so too are *you* as the perceiv*er* of the *mirage*.

DO NOT TAKE THE DREAM AS YOURS

NISARGADATTA MAHARAJ

One of the classic errors in the "it's all an illusion" or "it's all a dream" is that the perceiv*er* of the illusion or dream, respectively, does not appreciate that they are part of the dream or illusion itself.

The perceiv*er*, experienc*er*, know*er*, observ*er* of the dream is part of the *dream-mirage*. Once this has been "*gotten*" or *apperceived* - this is *waking up*.

The realization that you are a *mirage*, (*along with everything else*), *who does not know you are a mirage*, strikes to the core of the issue. For if you believe **YOU ARE** or **I AM**, then, the illusion or *mirage* is separate from you. Then, not only **YOU ARE** – but **IT IS**. As long as **I AM** or **YOU ARE** then **IT IS**.

Once there is an awakening to the **I AM, YOU ARE**, as the vehicle for **CONSCIOUSNESS** which acts as the glue which holds together the *mirage*, all vanishes upon investigation like a *mirage* of water on the desert; to repeat again.

WHATEVER CONCEPTS YOU HAVE COLLECTED IN THIS WORLD ARE TOTALLY USELESS. UNDERSTAND THAT THE TOTAL MANIFESTATION IS THE CHILD OF A BARREN WOMAN.

NISARGADATTA MAHARAJ
(PG. 43, Consciousness And The Absolute)

Concepts are conceived. Since all conceiving is **CONSCIOUSNESS** only how can they help a "you" which is only made of **THAT ONE SUBSTANCE** or **UNDIFFERENTIATED CONSCIOUSNESS**. Believing that a concept can help a "you" is an illusion within an illusion. The first illusion is an imagined "you," the second is a concept about an imagined you. Both are made of **CONSCIOUSNESS** and are of this *mirage* world. When this is *apperceived*, it evaporates.

To appreciate this further. If **I AM** is intact then the *mirage which does not know it is a mirage* will want to get better, more healthy, worry about death, try to obtain knowledge etc., another student asked Maharaj about the future, he laughed,

NOW WE ARE MAKING THE WEDDING PLANS FOR THE CHILD OF A BARREN WOMAN

NISARGADATTA MAHARAJ

In this *mirage,* which is made of **CONSCIOUSNESS**, the concept of knowledge or ignorance arises. This knowledge or ignorance which arises is made of **CONSCIOUSNESS** only.

KNOWLEDGE

ALL KNOWLEDGE IS LIKE THE CHILD OF A BARREN WOMAN.

NISARGADATTA MAHARAJ
(PG. 112, Consciousness And The Absolute)

When Nisargadatta Maharaj says, *The child of a barren woman*, he means that they do not exist. It is only **CONSCIOUS-NESS** which appears and as a *mirage* which *does not know it is a mirage* makes a "you" and "them" appear to exist. *You are a mirage which does not know you are a mirage.*

Since there is only **CONSCIOUSNESS**, there is no knowledge or bondage, like the child of a barren woman.

ALL KNOWLEDGE IS CONTAINED WITHIN THE DREAM ONLY AND NOT VALID.

NISARGADATTA MAHARAJ

The evaporation of this **I AM** brings forth the *realization* that the **I AM** is a reflection of **CONSCIOUSNESS** and is a *mirage*. However, *if this is not apperceived then, "the optical illusion whereby reflected objects are seen as real continues."* As long as this **trance**, called **maya** continues, so too will all the illusions of the "you," "you" call "yourself."

YOU ARE AN ILLUSION, MAYA, AN IMAGINATION. . . .

NISARGADATTA MAHARAJ
(PG. 1, CONSCIOUSNESS AND THE ABSOLUTE)

You are a manifestation of **CONSCIOUSNESS** or that **ONE SUBSTANCE** dividing and subdividing itself.

THERE IS NO CAUSE. YOU MERELY DREAM THAT YOU ROAM ABOUT. . . REALIZE THAT IT IS NOT YOU WHO MOVES FROM DREAM TO DREAM BUT THE DREAMS FLOW BEFORE YOU AND YOU ARE THE IMMUTABLE WITNESS.

(PG. 333, I Am That)

NO CONNECTION

. . . THERE IS NO LINK BETWEEN THE REAL WORLD AND THE IMAGINING WORLD.

NISARGADATTA MAHARAJ
(PG. 1, CONSCIOUSNESS AND THE ABSOLUTE)

There is an illusion that there is some link, connection, or relationship between the unmanifest and manifest world. Does the *mirage* in a desert which is non-existent have anything really to do with the desert. In this way, do not look for connections, meaning, or the purpose between the manifest and unmanifest. If you do, this can lead one to believe in the illusion of cause-effect, and reincarnation.

Question: What about karma and reincarnation

ALL STORIES OF REINCARNATION AND REBIRTH ARE MERE STORIES MEANT FROM THE IGNORANT MASSES. . .

NISARGADATTA MAHARAJ

Stephen: There is only one substance. Karma and reincarnation are concepts within the *mirage* which seek to justify; and, in the end, ultimately only support a non-existent *mirage* character who believes he is caught in the illusion of existence..

THERE IS NO SUCH THING AS EXISTENCE OR NON-EXISTENCE.

NISARGADATTA MAHARAJ

The concept of existence or non-existence is a concept *born of a mirage which does not know it is a mirage.*

Since the *mirage* is an appearance or illusion between the dream subject (perceiver) and dream object (perceiv*ed*).

Both are part of the dream *mirage*, and, since they appeared - they disappear upon investigation and are NOT - there is no link to the real.

Is there a link between the desert and the imagined water. Only that the water appears to exist in or on the desert. You have identified with the non-existent water which disappears as "you" come closer and investigate it. Enquire by turning awareness upon itself. "I" used to think that when Maharaj said, *question* this, *explore* that, *find out* this or that, "I" imagined that "I" would "get" some knowledge or information. All "I" got was that the "it" that was being investigated and "I" didn't exist, that "it" and *"I" were not*. In the same way, question everything in the *mirage* until it vanishes, then question the question*er* too then it will evaporate.

I KNOW NOTHING.
ALL KNOWLEDGE IS IN DREAM ONLY
AND NOT VALID.

NISARGADATTA MAHARAJ

The experienc*er*, like the experience itself, is made of **CONSCIOUSNESS. CONSCIOUSNESS**, is the substance that the *mirage* is made of.

In this way, any experience and its experienc*er* are made of **CONSCIOUSNESS** and part of the *mirage*.

Question: But certainly *"I"* can change or choose.

Stephen: There is no free will to change or choose, because there is only **CONSCIOUSNESS** - *no you*. Any attempt to turn yourself into a better person is ridiculous, it is like a shadow or *mirage* trying to be a better *mirage*.

THERE IS ONLY ONE TRUTH
IN THE WORLD AND THAT IS
THAT EVERYTHING IS UNREAL

NISARGADATTA MAHARAJ
(PG. 63, Consciousness And The Absolute)

What is apparently happening is unreal. This brings us to one of the major confusions in one of the most important teachings of **ADVAITA-VEDANTA**, and (**NISARGA YOGA**) the yoga of Nisargadatta Maharaj, namely I am not the doer. This approximation leaves us or implies there is a doer, that just isn't us that is doing. Call the doer GOD, VOID or whatever. It is like the old saying — Thy Will Be Done. This makes no sense. It implies, a Thy, a will and a BIG DOER. How can this be with only **ONE SUBSTANCE**.

WHATEVER IS SUPPOSEDLY HAPPENING IS AN
ILLUSION. NOTHING IS REALLY HAPPENING
BECAUSE THE BASIC CONCEPT BEINGNESS
IS ITSELF AN ILLUSION.

NISARGADATTA MAHARAJ
(PG. 200, Seeds Of Consciousness)

What must be emphasized rather than I am not the doer which implies a BIG DOER is - *There is no doer or doing or done.* This is more precise and it reveals the nature of the *mirage*.

A doer appears after the fact within the brain's cerebral cortex (which is part of the *mirage*) which creates the concept and declares doership after the fact. To believe what the cerebral cortex says or produces is like believing a *mirage* (thought) produced by a *mirage*, the cerebral cortex.

Most importantly, doer, doing, and done are only occur-
rences within the *mirage* itself. Once, the substratum or substance
namely **CONSCIOUSNESS** is *apprehended*, there is *no I, thou,
or other*, and hence *no doer - doing - done*.

THE ORIGINAL ILLUSION GOES ON

THE ORIGINAL ILLUSION. . .
WILL NOT STOP ACTING. YOU CANNOT REMOVE
THE ORIGINAL ILLUSION—IT HAS
TO CONTINUE, SUBSEQUENT ILLUSIONS
YOU CAN REMOVE, BUT NOT THE
ORIGINAL ILLUSION

NISARGADATTA MAHARAJ
(PG. 186, Seeds Of Consciousness)

Most people have had the idea than "when" "I" realize,
everything stops - the dream ends. This is not the case. The original *mirage* of **CONSCIOUSNESS** remains and continues; However, the substratum or substance of which it is all made, reveals
itself, so that the perceiv*er*-perceiv*ed* are one **CONSCIOUSNESS**
and one awakens from the dream of duality.

YOU WILL SEE GRASS GROWING,
WATER FLOWING IN RIVERS,
WAVES ON THE OCEAN, ETC., THAT IS
THE ORIGINAL MAYA—YOU CAN'T STOP THAT.

NISARGADATTA MAHARAJ
(PG. 186, Seeds Of Consciousness)

NO REALITY

JANESHWAR SAID WHATEVER EXISTS HAS NO SUBSTANCE, IT IS UNREAL.

NISARGADATTA MAHARAJ
(PG. 44, The Ultimate Medicine)

Although Janeshwar Maharaj calls **CONSCIOUSNESS** the *divine substance*, simultaneously, he understands that if it exists, it exists only as a *mirage*. Because all existence is *mirage* based. In this way, ultimately, even the concept of the *mirage* being made of **CONSCIOUSNESS** is only true in the context of the *mirage* self. Therefore, existence, and even **CONSCIOUSNESS** itself is part of the *mirage* and unreal.

All is part of the dream and all *knowledge or ignorance - both have no validity* and need to be investigated and discarded.

Question: If everything is a *mirage*, what are these spiritual experiences I have?

Stephen: Not only is everything a *mirage*, you are a *mirage* not *getting* that you are a *mirage*. All "experiences" are experienced by a *mirage person* having experiences.

WHATEVER THE EXPERIENCER FEELS OR THINKS IS ALL IN CONSCIOUSNESS AND IS NOT REAL.

NISARGADATTA MAHARAJ
(PG. 67, Consciousness And The Absolute)

Question: This sounds like I am a virtual reality.

Stephen: *You are a mirage that does not know you are a mirage.* The glue that holds the *mirage* together is **I AM**. As long as you believe **I AM** and do not *apperceive* the **CONSCIOUSNESS** which the **I AM** is made of, then the *mirage* remains solid and the world and you are upside down.

Question: I have been a Fourth Way Gurdjieff student for twenty years and this sounds like Gurdjieff.

Stephen: Gurdjieff used the metaphor of the kundabuffer that was installed in you that the world is upside down. This metaphor means that all experiences are in **CONSCIOUSNESS** and in space-time. In other words, in order to have a you an **I AM**, experiences etc., you have to have the physics dimensions and forces, the concept of location etc. All of what you call "you" and "I" are based on an experienc*er* having experiences. There is no experienc*er* separate from the experience. This all appears to occur in space-time because of an **I AM** which appears to exist in space-time and in a specific location. Gurdjieff's kundabuffer is **I AM** although it was not installed, it is the **I AM** which makes the unreal seem real.

Question: Wow!

Stephen: Now, what occurs is that you discover that not only is **I AM** the glue which holds together the *mirage*, but *experiences occur within and are part of the mirage-dream character only.* Therefore, everything is backward. What you experience is part of the *mirage-dream.* Even the perceiv*er* and know*er* of the *mirage* who is seeking enlightenment or the enlightened experience or freedom is in the *mirage* itself.

... IT IS FROM THIS ENTITY FICTION THAT FREEDOM IS SOUGHT.

NISARGADATTA MAHARAJ

Question: Is everything unreal?

Stephen: Everything in space-time and all experiences are part of the *mirage* and are unreal. All you are and know about are unreal.

Question: So what I thought was real was unreal?

Stephen: All experiences are *mirage*-dream based and are unreal. No experiences within **I AM** and space-time are real - it is all reversed. This is why Nisargadatta Maharaj when asked who are you? replied,

NOTHING PERCEIVABLE OR CONCEIVABLE.

NISARGADATTA MAHARAJ

Question: What about **CONSCIOUSNESS**.

Stephen: **CONSCIOUSNESS** is what the **I AM** is made of. It is what the *mirage*-dream body is made of—no **CONSCIOUSNESS**—no *mirage* dream-body—no **CONSCIOUSNESS**—no **I AM.**

Question: Yet you say everything is **UNDIFFERENTIATED CONSCIOUSNESS.**

Stephen: Only within the *mirage.* Once **CONSCIOUSNESS** "realizes" there is only **CONSCIOUSNESS**, then

there is no *mirage* and no such thing as **CON-
SCIOUSNESS**.

Question: But am I not **CONSCIOUSNESS**

Stephen: The **I AM** is made of **CONSCIOUSNESS**, the "I"
              you call yourself is a reflection of **CONSCIOUS-
              NESS,** which also reflects the **I AM** which is a *mi-
              rage. There is no person.* The person and the body
              you imagine yourself to be is a reflection of **CON-
              SCIOUSNESS** through the original *mirage* appear-
              ance called **I AM**.

Question: **I AM NOTHINGNESS?**

Stephen: Stay there.

IN THE ORIGINAL NON-BEING STATE
I DID NOT KNOW THE SENSE OF BEING

(PG. 43, Nectar Of Immortality)

Question: But aren't spiritual paths coming from GOD or Gu-
              rus and not part of the *mirage*?

Stephen: No, even spirituality, spiritual paths, Gods, Gurus
              and dieties are all part of the *mirage*.

ALL PATHS LEAD TO UNREALITY.
PATHS ARE CREATIONS WITHIN THE SCOPE OF
KNOWLEDGE; THEREFORE, PATHS AND
MOVEMENTS CANNOT TRANSPORT YOU INTO
REALITY, BECAUSE THEIR FUNCTION IS TO
ENMESH YOU WITHIN THE DIMENSIONS OF
KNOWLEDGE, WHILE REALITY PREVAILS
PRIOR TO IT.

NISARGADATTA MAHARAJ
(THE ULTIMATE MEDICINE)

Epilogue

· ·

STAY IN THE I AM, LET GO OF EVERYTHING ELSE.

NISARGADATTA MAHARAJ

This simple statement contains it all. **BE** the non-verbal **I AM** of no thoughts, memory, emotions, associations, perceptions, attention or intentions, let go of everything else. This **I AM**, is the Guru, **GOD**, and although the **I AM** is the the glue which holds the mirage together, it is through the **I AM** *mirage* that **CONSCIOUS-NESS** reflects out all we think we are, know, and the world around us. In this way, everything, including the **I AM** is made of **CON-SCIOUSNESS**. Once the *mirage* of the **I AM** is "there" it acts like glue holding "your" world together. To meditate on **GOD** is to meditate on **I AM** which acts like a gateway to the **CONSCIOUS-NESS** that the **I AM** is made of. And it is from **I AM** that upon its evaporation "you" are propelled into the *apperception prior* to **CONSCIOUSNESS** itself.

In the late seventies,, I asked Nisargadatta Maharaj, "I cannot stop coming here, what is this desire," Nisargadatta Maharaj replied, "you have won the grace of your true nature." I then asked him, "does it matter in what form this grace comes?" He replied:

"YOU THINK YOU ARE A PERSON SO YOU THINK MAHARAJ IS A PERSON, YOU THINK YOU ARE AN ENTITY OR A DEITY, SO YOU THINK MAHARAJ IS AN ENTITY OR A DEITY. MAHARAJ IS NOT A PERSON, AN ENTITY OR A DEITY MAHARAJ IS COSMIC CONSCIOUSNESS."

Years later "I" realized the truth of this statement.

QUESTION: THE LONGING TO BREAK THE SHELL,WHERE DOES IT COME FROM?

MAHARAJ: FROM.THE UNMANIFESTED.

(PG. 356, I Am That)

So like a child in pain I asked so many questions of him, which he answered so clearly, directly and powerfully that even now "I" marvel at their power and direct simplicity. So where does one go to receive this understanding?

THE TRUE REFUGE IS IN THE UNMANIFESTED. . .

(PG. 325, I Am That)

And how long will it take?

. . . YOU WILL GET MATURITY QUICKLY IF YOU WOULD STAY PUT IN YOUR NOTHINGNESS

NISARGADATTA MAHARAJ

As the **I AM** evaporates, at first "you" realize "your" own **NOTHINGNESS**, then even the **NOTHINGNESS** and the awar*er* of the **NOTHINGNESS** evaporates in **VOID OF UNDIFFER-ENTIATED NOTHINGNESS**.

. . . BEING NOTHING I AM ALL NOTHING IS ME IS THE FIRST STEP. EVERYTHING IS ME IS THE NEXT. . . .

NISARGADATTA MAHARAJ
(PG. 518, I Am That)

Two questions arise from this. The first is, how to stay in the **I AM**?

TRACE EVERY ACTION TO ITS SELFISH MOTIVE, AND LOOK AT THE MOTIVE INTENTLY UNTIL IT DISSOLVES.

NISARGADATTA MAHARAJ
(PG. 315, I Am That)

By tracing everything back through the False Self, we land in **I AM**. And, second, what is the **I AM** of no thoughts, memory, emotions, associations, perception, attention or intensions?

THE I AM IS THIS WORLD
MATERIALIZED OUT OF NOTHINGNESS.

NISARGADATTA MAHARAJ

(PG. 43, The Nectar Of Immortality)

And as **THAT** "becomes" the **I AM** and this, and this **I AM** "becomes" **THAT** "we" move into and out of and through the divine pulsation or throb, called in Sanskrit **SPANDA**.

What we call this universe is a throb, a **SPANDA**, a pulsation, nothing more, as the form becomes **EMPTINESS, EMPTINESS** becomes form.

What words does **I AM THAT I AM**. Describe?

How can we trace this process? With whatever is being experienced trace it back to the non-verbal **I AM** of no thoughts, memory, emotions, associations, perceptions, attention or intentions, until the **I AM** itself evaporates as the **CONSCIOUSNESS,** which the **I AM** is made of, reveals itself. Soon, "when" that **CONSCIOUSNESS** is all there is, then there is only **NOTHINGNESS**.

THE KNOWLEDGE I AM
IS NOTHING

(PG. 36, The Nectar of Immortality)

The **I AM** is made of **NOTHINGNESS**, pure **CONSCIOUSNESS** condensed. But **I AM** is an illusion of **CONSCIOUSNESS,** and **CONSCIOUSNESS** once it realizes itself is **NOTHINGNESS** only.

Do not be deluded into imagining there is an answer to **WHO AM I**; or I will find out **WHO I AM**, because you won't because **THERE IS NO I THAT YOU ARE. ALL "I's" EVAPORATE.**

So how does one end this tribute? When I go back in memory to that most remarkable room, which Nisargadatta Maharaj sat and answered questions in for decades, it seems unbelievable and I have no words to describe my gratitude. For, even now, almost 20 years after his departure— the purest, most direct, most confrontive teachings continue to continue.

From a small attic in a slum of Bombay, where around the corner were the infamous "cages" where prostitutes were caged and sold, arose, Maruti Kampli who dissolved to become Nisargadatta Maharaj.

Like a lotus arising out of mud, Nisargadatta Maharaj, like no other, never compromised nor did he play anyone's game.

To paraphrase Shakespeare's "Hamlet," "To thy own self be true, and when you are true to yourself, you are true to everyone else." So was Nisargadatta Maharaj, a lotus of truth, arising out of the mud. His teachings were so direct and confrontative, that all that was untrue and false shattered like a glass house in the wind of a storm. And upon the shattering of the glass house, the space "inside," so obvious to Maharaj, yet so invisible to "me," was forever freed.

Nisargadatta Maharaj once asked someone, "Who told you, you exist? When there was no reply, he said, "**CONSCIOUSNESS** tells you you exist, and you believe it, if you understand just this it is enough."

So the child of a barren women offers this tribute to Nisargadatta Maharaj, another child of a barren woman. And to everyone reading this book who too is the child of a barren woman in honor of **THAT**

And what is **THAT**?

THE WORD THAT
IN THE STATEMENT REFERS TO
EVERYTHING THAT IS IN
THE TOTALITY.

NISARGADATTA MAHARAJ

With Love
        Your brother
                Stephen

REFERENCES AND RECOMMENDED READING

. . . .

Balsekar, Ramesh, Pointers from Nisargadatta Maharaj, 1982 Acorn Press, Durham NC

Edited-Dunn, Jean, Consciousness and the Absolute, 1994 Acorn Press, Durham, NC

_____, Prior to Consciousness, 1985, Durham Press, NC

_____, Seeds of Consciousness, 1982, Grove Press Inc., NY

Edited - Powell, Robert, The Nectar of the Lord's Feet , 1987. Element Books, England. Later published as, The Nectar of Immortality, Blue Dove Press, San Diego, CA, 1997.

_____, The Ultimate Medicine, Blue Dove Press , San Diego, CA, 1994

_____, The Experience of Nothingness, Blue Dove Press, San Diego, CA, 1996

Nisargadatta Maharaj, I AM THAT 1973, Chetana Books, Bombay, Acorn Press, Durham NC

Osborne, Arthur, The Collected Works of Ramana Maharshi, Samuel Weiser Inc., York Beach, Maine

U.G. Krishnamurti, The Mystique of Enlightenment:, The Unrational Ideas of a Man called U.G., Coleman Publishing, New York 1984

U.G. Krishnamurti, The Courage to Stand Alone, Plover Press, NY 1997

U.G. Krishnamurti, The Mind is Myth:, Disquieting Conversations with, the Man called U.G., Dinesh Publications 1988, India.

Venkatesanawda, Swami The Supreme Yoga, Chiltern Yoga Trust, Australia, 1976.

RECOMMENDED READING

Singh J., Pratyabhijnahrdeyam:, The Secret Of Self Recognition , Delhi India, Motilal Banasidas, .1963

_____, Siva Sutra: The Yoga , Of Supreme Identity, Delhi: India, Motilal Banasidas, 1979

_____ , Vijnanabhairava, Divine Consciousness, Delhi: India, Motilal Banasidas, 1979

_____, Spanda karikas: , Lessons In the Divine Pulsation, Delhi: India, Motilal Banasidas, 1980

Hua Master Tripatika Surangama Sutra, San Francisco (1980), Buddhist Text Translation Society

Wolinsky, Stephen, Quantum Consciousness - 1993, Bramble Books

Wolinsky, Stephen, Tao of Chaos, 1994, Bramble Books

Wolinsky, Stephen, The Way of the Human Vol. I, Quantum Institute – 1999, Capitola, CA

Wolinsky, Stephen, The Way of the Human Vol. II, Capitola, CA - 1999

Wolinsky, Stephen, The Way of the Human Vol. III, Capitola, CA - 1999

Wolinsky, Stephen, Hearts On fire: The Tao Of Meditation, Capitola, CA 1995

BOOKS OF RELATED INTEREST

DANCING WITH THE VOID

The Innerstandings of a Rare-born Mystic

Sunyata

ISBN: 81-7822-134-9

TEN UPANISHADS OF FOUR VEDAS

Ram K. Piparaiya

ISBN: 81-7822-159-4

DIALOGUES ON REALITY

An Exploration into the Nature of Our Ultimate Identity

Robert Powell

ISBN: 81-7822-140-3

SATISFYING OUR INNATE DESIRE

Roy Eugene Davis

ISBN: 81-7822-198-5

COME, COME, YET AGAIN COME

Osho

ISBN: 81-7822-154-3

SILENCE SPEAKS

Baba Hari Dass

ISBN: 81-7822-172-1

YOU ARE NOT

Beyond the Three Veils of Consciousness

Stephen Wolinsky

ISBN: 81-7822-261-2

PATH WITHOUT FORM

A Journey into the Realm Beyond Thought

Robert Powell

ISBN: 81-7822-135-7

GETTING TO WHERE YOU ARE

The Life of Meditation

Steven Harrison

ISBN: 81-7822-202-7

KARMA AND CHAOS

New and Collected Essays on Vipassana Meditation

Paul R. Fleischman

ISBN: 81-7822-177-2

SUPERCONSCIOUSNESS

How to Benefit from Emerging Spiritual Trends

J. Donald Walters

ISBN: 81-7822-026-1

CAN YOU LISTEN TO A WOMAN

A Man's Journey to the Heart

David Forsee

ISBN: 81-7822-112-8